Greetings! I would like to introduce Lisa Heidrich to you...I have attended several small group studies and retreats lead by Lisa. Her material is fresh, well researched, creative, relevant, and always has a welcome dash of humor. I highly recommend Lisa as a dynamic, energetic speaker with a heart for the LORD and for women.

~Lindy Scherffius, Area Representative — Stonecroft Ministries

Pick up this book and you'll be grabbing the tool that will get you over any obstacle that is hindering your public speaking—even if you don't fully understand what's holding you back! Lisa's perspective motivates while her questions walk you through fear into confidence when speaking in front of even the largest of crowds!

~Curtis Martin MBA, Executive Sales Training, Veteran Commissioned Officer, USAF

Lisa Heidrich is a refreshing voice in an assorted realm of speakers & authors. She approaches her craft with an organic earthiness, giving her an instant rapport with everyday women. Lisa's candid confessions about her life experiences unite her with diverse audiences, allowing them to connect better relationally & through their identity as daughters in Christ.

~Nichole Broome, singer/songwriter, www.nicholebroome.com

I've had the pleasure of serving alongside of Lisa in ministry and have been so impressed with her sweet spirit and her passionate love for our Lord! Her authenticity and ability to connect with women is so refreshing. Any organization would be privileged to have her serve them, whether it be as a speaker, writer or voice over talent. She always gives all she's got into what she does and the glory is always directed at her Heavenly Father!

~Leslie Nease, Speaker, Writer, "His Radio Morning Show" Co-Host

Speaking Confidence

Lisa C. Bongiorno-Heidrich

Chalfont House
ChalfontHouse.com
Dumfries, Virginia

Speaking Confidence
Published by Chalfont House Publishing
PO Box 84, Dumfries, VA 22026
www.ChalfontHouse.com

Scripture quoted by permission. Quotations designated (NIV) are from THE HOLY BIBLE: NEW INTERNATIONAL VERSION®. NIV®. Copyright © 1973, 1978, 1984 by Biblica. All rights reserved worldwide.

Scripture quotations designated (The Message) are from THE MESSAGE: The Bible in Contemporary Language copyright 2002 by Eugene Peterson. Used by permission of NavPress. All rights reserved. www.NavPress.com

Scripture quotations marked (Amplified Bible) are taken from the Amplified® Bible, Copyright © 1954, 1958, 1962, 1964, 1965, 1987 by The Lockman Foundation. Used by permission. (www.Lockman.org)

Scripture quotations marked (NLT) are taken from the Holy Bible, New Living Translation, copyright 1996. Used by permission of Tyndale House Publishers, Inc., Wheaton, Illinois 60189. All rights reserved.

Cover photo of hands and microphone, ©iStockphoto.com/RapidEye

ISBN 978-1-938708-03-9 (paperback)
ISBN 978-1-938708-04-6 (ebook)
ISBN 978-1-938708-05-3 (audiobook)

Published in the United States by Chalfont House Publishing.

Dedication:
This book is dedicated to my Savior Jesus,
who saved me from myself when no religion could.

For my sons Matthew and Christopher,
may you always speak confidence
in all you say and into those you speak to.
I love you dearly.

Acknowledgments

Lynellen, thank you for taking my words and thoughts and synthesizing them into a coherent manuscript. Our phone calls every Friday at 2:00 PM were a moment of inspiration and direction. Your impact on my life has been one that will stay in my heart and on my work for years to come. You are one special and talented lady!

My deep heartfelt thanks to my family for their encouragement and grace during the process of book writing your support has carried me through.

Melissa, my sister, for reviewing and helping me with grammar and writing technicalities. You are gifted and I appreciate you. I remember those early days of reading to you and coaching you with your elocution. I see how those days led me to these days and have enjoyed the journey.

Pam, your endless patience in designing and assisting me with getting my image out there. You are a real artist, from photographs to business cards, and a very dear blessing. I am grateful for you.

For all the Stonecroft Volunteers, staff and friends who have brought me to where I am today as a speaker. Your amazing prayers, guidance, and perseverance have changed my life for all eternity. How I adore you all from the MidSouth Division and SCM nation.

My special thanks for the book review team (Jeff and Curtis). Thank you for your honesty and for investing your time and effort into my book.

Last, but not least, to my mom Marge, for her years of instilling into me the idea of "never giving up" and how powerfully we can speak and have others hear our voice, even in silence. Love you.

"We thank you God, we thank you. Your NAME is our favorite Word.

Your mighty deeds are all we have to brag about" – Psalm 75 :1 (The Message)

Phases of Developing Speaking Confidence

Introduction & Welcome
Stand Up and Say Your Piece

While meeting people in various places, especially writing conferences, retreats and workshops, I have found that many people already have the material they desire to communicate but they simply are not confident enough to speak it. Some are fearful, some need more information, and some never realized they could speak. This is a hands-on book filled with purpose and action. It is designed to guide you into an avenue you may not have experienced previously: Speaking Confidence. Confidence is the central message I hope to impart. Each chapter suggests action steps that encourage you to move forward into confidence, no matter how daunting the task may seem. You *can* do this. Will you try?

Confidence is realizing that you are gifted in a marvelous way and others need to hear from you. I want you to have Confidence in knowing that:

- There is no one else in this world like you,
- What you say sounds differently than anyone else in this world, and
- No one else in this world has your material, speech, talk, prayer, or the power to share this content with the world like you do.

Even though I have twenty years of experience as a public speaker, I still remember what it feels like to shake in my shoes before a live audience. I recall as a teenager I delivered various texts in front of a congregation of two hundred on a weekly basis: from announcements to narratives, readings and teachings. As a nursing professor, I prepared academic speeches for classes of students. Over the past decade, I have traveled to hundreds of groups annually and shared my thoughts as an International keynote speaker at conferences, workshops and live web streaming global conversations reaching 10,000 attendees. Another way I have honed my skills and gleaned experience is by providing narration for audio books and voice-over work for countless commercials in the radio industry. I have also had the great privilege of working with dozens of people one-on-one as a speaking coach to help them achieve their confidence.

The ART of Speaking

Speaking is an art form and there are many opportunities to share your voice. One of my passions has always been working with others and encouraging their elocution. I consider myself a vocal performance motivator, a coach, a Body of Christ Activist, a global conversationalist, and someone who wants to encourage you to climb over any barriers keeping you from public speaking, whether the audience is 1 person or 10,001 people. If an extroverted introvert like me can do this, so can you.

We have all been designed to communicate. Our "VOICE" is seen and heard in varying formats but no two will ever look the same or sound identical. Have you ever thought about what your "VOICE" might be? Now is the time to share that private, quiet, hidden-away voice with others around you. This book will inspire your confidence to speak about what you have written or thought. I want to encourage the authentic delivery of your ideas or written work.

Please, do not throw the book down yet! I am here to encourage you to explode into the 'you' that was created with gifts and ingredients making you uniquely you. You have a magnificent voice. My purpose is to connect you with your sound. I desire to assist you in minimizing any challenge that holds you back. I pray that in this book you will find the encouragement and the motivation to stand up and say what you desire to say with comfortable confidence. As

you begin to read and experience the content of this
you step by step, phase by phase, from fearful to f
speaking endeavors.

Now may I share a little confidential information? I am not
the most confident person you might meet. I have been socially
trained to be personable, but sometimes all my efforts yield little. I
have my hang-ups and shortcomings and some days my confidence
stays packed away in solitude. Therefore, you and I may have a few
things in common.

However...

I have assurance because I believe in something bigger and
better than myself. Prayer and trust in a living and listening God who
lavishly loves instills confidence into each of us as needed. Drop by
drop, ounce by ounce. My prayer is that this book touches everyone
needing inspiration and gives them the information they require to
stand composed and speak with confidence, in addition to speaking
confidence into others in their world. What we give, we receive.

Life Stories from Real People

I have a favorite speaking story I like to share. It's about a
dude from a long time ago. His name was Jeremiah. No last name,
just Jeremiah. Some of you may know of him but for others this story
might be one you are discovering for the very first time. Either way,
it is an important story and on my heart to share. This is a true and
authentic Bible story from the prophet Jeremiah, Chapter 1 (emphasis mine throughout the translation of the NIV and the paraphrase of
The Message). It goes like this...

There was a creator, His Name, God, who said, "Before I formed
you in the womb, I knew you, before you were born, I knew you, before you
saw the light of day for the first time I had huge & holy plans for you; **I set you
apart**. I appointed you as a speaker to the nations, that is what I had in mind
for you."

Jeremiah replied, "Hang on, hold on there God, Oh Sovereign Lord, ait — a — minute, I do NOT know how to speak; I don't know anything; I am only a child."

God replied, "Do not say you are only a child, don't say you are only this or only that, no excuses here. You MUST go to everyone I send you and say and speak whatever I tell you to say. I'll tell you where you are to go and you will go there. Go to everyone and don't be afraid, for I am with you. Do not fear a soul, for I'll rescue you, I'll be with you, I'll be right there looking after you. I will even give you the very words to speak!"

Then you know what happened? The Bible says, "God reached out His Hand and touched Jeremiah's lips, his entire mouth, hand delivered! See today, this day **I appoint you over nations, people and governments, I've given you a job to speak up and speak out**, today is a red-letter day. Stand up and say your piece!"

Stand up and say your piece. How do those words make you feel? How do you feel about those words? Do you believe them? What are the excuses you might give your friends, family, yourself or God for not standing up and saying your piece? Would you be brazen enough or frightened enough to argue back saying, "But…but… I don't have the time. I cannot create a website. My voice shakes. I might cry. I am too nervous. No one wants to hear me. Heck, I don't even have any business cards. I cannot be a speaker, that is a crazy idea!" Everyone has excuses that hold us back. As your new personal Speaking Coach I respond, "Find a better excuse. Better yet, STOP blocking what you have been called to do. I will repeat it one more time: STAND UP and please SAY your piece."

That is my prayer for each reader. Simply stand up and say your piece. I hope you acknowledge that God has your back. He will supply the words when you cannot find them. I also hope that you will trust and believe in something bigger, stronger, and higher then yourself at work here. The God who created this universe will touch your lips today and inspire in you the confidence to speak the message with which He has so richly blessed you. Jeremiah was a regular person just like you and me. He was shy once, he was hesitant twice, and he wanted to hide forever. He spoke back to God and he was shaken. He stood up to speak back to the Almighty. Imagine that. This is a true story and I invite you to investigate it and live it. Starting today, may you start *Speaking Confidence* in each and every word you speak.

Welcome! I am so glad you are here.

 -Lisa

Phase 1.0 — Communicating
Writing vs. Speaking

You're holding this book for a purpose and a reason: It's part of your calling to share your ideas and to expose what you think, feel, learn, and pray. As a blogger, letter writer, emailer, list maker, card sender, freelance, or professional writer, you have already honed and sharpened your skills as a communicator via the written word. That is by far the more tedious mechanism of communication. Now you have a desire to speak. Excellent, you're in the right place. Maybe it's an assignment for work, a necessity for promoting your book, or a self-improvement idea. As an author, teacher, or individual who wants to become more active in public speaking, the truth is the more you engage in public conversations, the more you develop your abilities as a speaker.

I have a huge secret to share with you: You already have your speaking material, your message. You know what to say. Some of you have even recorded or written it out into journals, books, CDs, MP3s, voice recorders, articles, reports, prayers, or blogs.

Write about it: In what medium have you recorded your message? What is your writing and/or speaking genre? Circle all that apply.

Blog	Video Log (vlog)	Letters
Emails to individuals	Email newsletter	Cards
Twitter	Social media	Fiction novel
Journal	Magazine article	Short story
Newspaper article	Academic papers	Non-fiction book
Lecture	Sermon	Workshop
Comedy routine	Speech	Voice mail
Audio book	TV show	Radio show

Other writing and/or speaking genres you employ:

_____

_____

_____

_____

1.1 Sharing Your Voice

Speaking is an organic communication tool created inside us. Speaking is easier than writing. As infants, we learn to speak by imitating the sounds of the voices around us. There are no special classes to teach us how to speak. By cooing and babbling as babies, we exercise our vocal chords from whispers to screams. It isn't until pre-K or kindergarten that we are taught to write. We speak before we write. Last I checked there was no core curriculum or mandate that requires young children to take any speaking classes unless they have an identifiable diagnosed impediment, speaking disorder or handicap. Hang with me here just a moment. If you have deciphered what I just wrote, you now realize that you have mastered the more difficult form of communication: writing versus speaking. Congratulations, you are ahead of the game.

Speaking is something we all do on a daily basis. Some of you out there might whisper, "This is the world of technology!! We do not have to speak every day." I'd like to push back on that just a bit. We have a choice. Even with all the communication tools (computers, cell phones, smart devices, and social media) available, still most of us cannot go a full day without speaking to something or someone, including yourself. Whether you talk in person, chat with someone on the phone, or tell your pet to sit/stay/hush, you are speaking. I know from my own speaking history, that after a few days of speaking and teaching tours I'm ready for quiet. I have spoken my 30,000 words a day and I need recuperation time so I choose to speak very little. Speaking is just a natural action for us as humans and some days, yes it is a choice.

Speaking, talking, and communicating are part of our survival here on planet Earth. When was the last time you ordered fast food? You drive up to the menu, *speak* your order, someone receives it, an exchange of money takes place and you drive away. There are no touch screen order pads (*yet*). Waiters and waitresses are still gainfully employed. Most are still sporting a pad and pen, for heaven's sake! Maybe one day we will "touch screen" everything!

How many people do you speak to when you visit your doctor? Add it up...I'll wait. From my observation and calculations, for a regular medical doctor visit the average person will speak to and interact with approximately ten people from booking the appointment to filling the prescription at the pharmacy. I am including every word spoken, including short conversations like: *That will be fine, Sure, OK, Thank YOU, Yes, No, What did you say Dr.? That hurts, ouch!*...etc. We communicate through speech for survival.

Exercise: Grab a broom, wooden spoon, hammer, or remote control and use it like a microphone. Three times today, speak directions, compliments, or encouragement into your pretend microphone.

Write about it: How does your voice sound to you? Circle all that apply.

Appealing	Breathy	Brittle
Croaky	Unemotional	Flat
Grating	Gravelly	Gruff
Guttural	High-pitched	Hoarse
Husky	Matter-of-fact	Monotonous
Nasal	Quiet	Ringing
Rough	Shrill	Singsong
Soft-spoken	Strangled	Thick
Wheezy	Wobbly	Booming

Other descriptive words:

_____

_____

_____

Speaking is not something to be afraid of! You're wired and equipped for it already! I mean that sincerely. Try to receive those words and let them resonate in your head. My goal is to remove the obstacles that are keeping you from speaking with your best vocal performance. Let me help develop your confidence, comfort, and calmness as a speaker. There is absolutely nothing to be afraid of. Trust me.

Speaking is like exercising and developing a muscle. The more you practice, the stronger you become. So build your comfort zone by conversing with people and by speaking in front of others. Step out and speak. Start somewhere, even with just a quiet, still small whisper. This is an action-based book. You have taken the first step toward speaking confidently by reading this book. You'll get more experience by doing each exercise and journaling answers to each writing prompt. I'm confident you can do it!

Exercise: Speak or read aloud to anyone who will be an audience, even if you have to talk to your dog, your cat, your baby, your car, or your favorite plant. Chose an audience that already appreciates you. You don't have to like it, just try it as an exercise.

Write about it: How did it make you feel to speak or read to your appreciative audience?

1.2 Gathering Guts

You know what you want to say; now all you need is the guts to say it publicly. I promise: you have guts. There are two types of speakers: lots of guts, and normal guts. How is that for simplification? We all have guts. Both types are excellent orators. You can choose to erase the past and start anew right now. We each are uniquely designed to have our own special significant confidence in speaking. It's time now to eliminate all "stinking thinking," because you are powerful through your own voice as you speak to others. What we think about, ponder over, and dwell on is what we deliver in our words. Decide today you are ready to make a change and you *will* speak confidently with the grace, power, and volume with which you were created to speak. Be committed to developing your speaking confidence. As you speak and use your voice to influence, ignite, and inspire others, remember you are in charge. Your confidence is about what you believe on the *inside.* You can do this, I believe in you. Your message is one we all want to hear.

Exercise: Get three index cards, write the following statements on each one, and place them in three strategic places like your bathroom mirror, your refrigerator, and the dashboard of your car.

"I am powerful through my own voice."

"No one has a voice like mine."

"I will speak with confidence everywhere I go today."

1.3 Motivating Words – Your Expression

As you have discovered, **my mission is to edify people, and rehabilitate speakers by encouraging them to be heard and not to fear.** As a world, we have bigger problems than to have the number one *fear* remain public speaking. For goodness sakes, what are we thinking? I want to bump that fear down to the bottom of the phobia list where it rightfully belongs. I hope you go out with confidence to share your voice among the nations to make a difference not only in your own life but also in the lives of others who hear you. Imagine if we never heard musicians sing? How empty would our lives be without those words, notes and emotions that touch us so deeply? Can you image a world without music? Your words are just as critical. What you say matters.

Even if your expressions just touch one person, it was worth it. If you've heard of the "starfish story" you know exactly where I am coming from. By throwing that one starfish back into its natural habitat, you save it from drying up on the beach. It is one less dead starfish. ONE matters. Your words might be the ones that keep someone else from drying up on their own personal beach. Remind your spouse they are exceptional. Tell your kids how intelligent they are. Encourage a neighbor for their outstanding help with your house painting effort. Share what you have to say. Our words to one another truly do matter.

Write about it: How will you convey confidence from the inside out so others notice and glean from it?

Write about it: What are the words you will use to speak confidence into others? Circle the words that speak to you most.

Brilliant	Beautiful	Outstanding
Wonderful	Terrific	Amazing
Creative	Unique	Precious
Important	Valuable	Vibrant
Intelligent	Articulate	Happy
Cheerful	Imaginative	Optimistic
Dazzling	Clever	Smart
Sharp	Whimsical	Witty
Breathtaking	Splendid	Super
Fabulous	Ace	Excellent
Outstanding	Superior	Handsome
Attractive	First-class	Expert
Exceptional	Advanced	Loved

List other meaningful descriptive and motivating words here:

Ancient Authentic Advice

"I'm determined to watch steps and tongue so they won't land me in trouble. I decided to hold my tongue as long as Wicked is in the room. "Mum's the word," I said, and kept quiet. But the longer I kept silence the worse it got— my insides got hotter and hotter. My thoughts boiled over; I spilled my guts."

Phase 2.0 – Speaking Phobia
Fearful to Fearless Public Speaking

Maybe you're sitting there saying, "But Lisa, I have stage fright. I don't do crowds. I'm a writer, not a speaker. I'm an introvert. I can't do this!"

I say, "Let's face your obstacles and barriers one at a time. You can do this. Really. No problem, chill."

I work with regular people, performers, managers, directors, professors and teachers who have "speaking phobia," otherwise known as glossophobia. Glossophobia might also be called speaking anxiety, performance anxiety or stage fright. Glossophobia is the number one phobia, hands down. You're not alone in that mentality. The good news is it is not a terminal malady and can be cured. This book will offer you the foundational information and the practice exercises to guide you toward comfortable, confident public speaking. Yes, you read that right. You can reduce your fears. You can focus on comfortable and confident speaking in *public* if you are willing to give it a try. Let's get started.

Here are the top ten global PHOBIAS:

#1 — Public Speaking or stage fright - Glossophobia

#2 — Death or end of life - Necrophobia

#3 — Spiders and other arachnids - Arachnophobia

#4 — Darkness or twilight - Scotophobia or Myctophobia

#5 — Heights, altitude or elevations - Acrophobia

#6 — People or social situations - Sociophobia

#7 — Flying - Aerophobia

#8 — Outside or open spaces - Agoraphobia

#9 — Lightning and thunder - Brontophobia

#10 — Confined small spaces or rooms - Claustrophobia

Why is speaking the number one phobia in our world, even ahead of the phobia of death? My guess is that, as a society, the *message of fear* of public speaking has been handed down over the millennium. From early childhood school experiences, we remember those negative encounters and the phobia gets passed along, repeatedly. I think that phobias are contagious, especially among the young. Hysteria is also transmittable. Check out the next world crisis, such as a public shooting or natural disaster, and read what the local psychologists report. In crisis and emotional scenarios, we respond as a group. Ever heard of the convergence theory, where crowds bring together like-minded thinking? What we are taught to believe, both theoretically and practically, forms and shapes our belief from the inside out. My optimism is that your journey through this book will ease those thoughts, beliefs and practices. My aspiration is to provide you with truth about public speaking and diminish the fear for you personally. Over time, person by person, this phobia will be lessened by education and through experience, realizing it really isn't "THAT BAD."

Being a speaker might mean you will have to overcome more than one concern or phobia. For me, my secret anxiety about traveling on a plane was something I needed to address when asked to speak and tour in non-local places. The power of a secret is keeping it quiet. Once a secret is exposed it loses its power to control and demotivate us. Of course, some secrets are precious and we treasure them in our hearts. Those are the keepers. The negative secrets have to go; they have no hold on you now. Now I am over my aerophobia and I am here to tell you that whatever you decide in your mind and your heart you can overcome. Speaking stress is real, but the level we escalate it to is completely up to us.

Write about it: What secret or secrets have you been allowing to marinate and hold you prisoner for too long?

Write about it: What are your spoken or unspoken FEARS about public speaking? Circle all that apply, then list every other obstacle you can conjure up.

Throat will go dry   Mind will go blank

Someone will heckle   Stuttering

Sounding unknowledgeable   Audience will walk out

Not know how to answer a question

Others:

2.1 Facts about Speaking Fears

Let's look at some facts about the fear of speaking.

FACT ONE: Surveys show that most people would rather die than talk in front of a live audience. 75% of the population experiences stress with the thought of speaking publicly, according to the World Health Organization. Men and women are pretty equally affected by glossophobia.

FACT TWO: Having some social skill aversions can be normal, but we must realize they can affect our careers, our relationships, and may influence our success if we fail to do anything about them. Now is a great time to do something about the obstacles you are facing. It is never too late to do something about it. A person is never too old or too young to overcome an obstacle that is keeping them from their dream.

FACT THREE: Both men and women have sought medical intervention in an attempt to gain control over their speaking distress. Some public speakers have turned to beta-blockers, anti-anxiety medications, and acupuncture or hypnosis therapy to find relief.

FACT FOUR: Social phobias often start with shyness in childhood or early adolescence and progress during the adolescence years.

FACT FIVE: Phobias are contagious — we catch them from our family, friends, and the influencers in our lives.

As a little girl, I used to be afraid of sleeping in the dark. I could not sleep unless my closet door was closed and a night light ON. You know the story. Until I actually confronted my fear of the "boogey man" in my closet, I believed *he was there*. I didn't know what he looked like, but in my mind I was compelled to believe in the fear of him.

My official definition of fear: Fear is something we ourselves feed into our psyche and birth into our reality.

The feeling of fear is unpleasant and causes us apprehension or an anticipation of danger. Have you heard this acronym for F.E.A.R.? False Evidence Appearing Real. It's funny what our mind allows us to remember—all those broken records whispering in our heads that sound real. A negative trigger elicits an "icky" feeling when something is said or done and causes the pit of your stomach to shudder in fear. Sometimes these insecurities are self-inflicted because we control our mantra, expression, stronghold, or idea that repeats in our head. However, FEAR is not real. Identifying the trigger (the somebody or something that inhibits us) is the beginning of personal victory.

Write about it: What words do you associate with FEAR? Circle all that apply.

terror	horror	burden
humiliation	concern	uneasiness
rejection	insecurity	discomfort
panic	pride	unease
alarm	perfectionism	fret
apprehension	concern	agony
worry	nightmare	fuss
distress	fright	angst
embarrassment	being scared	hesitation
dread	nervousness	imprisonment
stress	fixation	restriction
limitation	constraint	immobilization

Other words: _____

Now narrow down your list to the top three words you associate with FEAR. List them here:

1) _____

2) _____

3) _____

Of those three words, choose one word you most correlate with FEAR. Write it in the blank below to complete this sentence:

_____ is holding me back from public speaking.

2.2 Fear Busters

Now that you have disclosed one major hang-up, you have a positive choice: LET IT GO. Be free. You have the ability to eliminate that barrier now that you have recognized it. Conquer those thoughts and purge them here. Let them go now and move forward.

Write about it: You are fearLESS. Whisper to yourself, "I am FEAR-LESS." Say it aloud. How does that feel?

_____

_____

_____

_____

_____

_____

_____

_____

To combat glossophobia, work through these tips:

1. **Know your material.** Pick a topic you are interested in. Know more about it than you include in your speech. Use humor, personal stories and conversational language – that way you won't easily forget what to say.

2. **Practice.** Practice. Practice! Rehearse aloud with all equipment you plan on using. Revise as necessary. Work to control filler words like "uh" and "um." Practice, pause and breathe. Practice with a timer and allow time for the unexpected.

3. **Know your audience.** Greet some of the audience members as they arrive. It's easier to speak to a group of friends than to strangers.

4. **Know the room.** Arrive early. Walk around the speaking area and practice using the microphone and any visual aids.

5. **Relax.** Begin by addressing the audience. It buys you time and calms your nerves. Pause, smile and count to three before saying anything. ("One one-thousand, two one-thousand, three one-thousand." Pause. Begin.) Transform nervous energy into enthusiasm.

6. **Visualize yourself giving your speech.** Imagine yourself speaking, your voice loud, clear and confident. Visualize the audience clapping – it will boost your confidence.

7. **Realize that people want you to succeed.** Audiences want you to be interesting, stimulating, informative and entertaining. They're rooting for you. Consider yourself as a teacher and the audience your class. The students HAVE to take your class. The students have PAID to take your class. An audience is there to listen to a speaker. Being a speaker indicates that you have something say – that's why you are speaking. The audience is just there because that is the way speaking works. You speak. You have an audience. They want you there. They are present to

hear what you have to present. They are your fans or soon-to-be fans.

8. **Don't apologize for any nervousness** or problem – the audience probably never noticed it.

9. **Concentrate on the message – not the medium.** Focus your attention away from your own anxieties and concentrate on your message and your audience.

10. **Gain experience.** Mainly, your speech should represent you — as an authority and as a person. Experience builds confidence, which is the key to effective speaking. A Toastmasters club can provide the experience you need in a safe and friendly environment.

I have shared something important with you. You already have your material, the past is the past, your hang-ups are yours to hang up already, and an audience is there for you and they have insecurities too. Let it go and now just speak it!

You will accomplish absolutely anything you set your mind to. Make a personal goal. I wish you would make speaking publicly a goal in your life because you never know whose life you might change by the power of your spoken word. I also trust you will begin to speak confidence into the lives of others, especially your family and children. Start to develop those speaking muscles and edify the little ones as valuable and creative speakers. Let's raise a new generation of fearless spokespersons. Together, each of us can make a difference in the statistics that plague our world unnecessarily. Seriously. I am giving you a personal challenge to speak confidence into others and help eliminate the global phobia surrounding public speaking. There is power in this cause.

I can't wait to start hearing from those who may have otherwise stayed silent, never to share their voice and the unique gifts they were created to employ. Please feel free to send me a tweet (my Twitter handle is @LisaCHeidrich) or email (lisalisa114@gmail. com). There are bigger, more serious phobias for us to face in this life. If we allow public speaking fear, fright, or panic to destroy our youth, what happens to our next generation of people? What a tragedy if we allow that to happen.

Write about it: I want to change the world by removing speaking phobia. If you could change something in this world, what would it be?

Ancient Authentic Advice
I'm fearless no matter what. Who or what can get to me?

Phase 3.0 – Audience Authenticity
Reality and Truth About Who Hears You

You asked an important question: WHAT ABOUT THE AUDIENCE? OH...them! They're not the problem at all. Here's another secret: the audience is there to hear you speak. Does that make your heart flip? Yes, the audience *wants to hear you speak*. That is why they are there.

Have you ever been part of an audience? Of course you have, in school, at a concert, at a movie, play, lecture, etc. Have you ever studied an audience? I have. I have noted that the people who make up the audience are regular people. They arrive, pick a seat, and look at the speaker (sometimes).

Why does the idea of the audience frighten us? Someone told us they are frightening and overwhelming. That is how rumors start! Let's completely stop any rumors, right now.

Write about it: How did you get the idea that audiences are mean, hurtful, dangerous, and nausea inducing?

3.1 Show & Tell

What gets our heart pounding about speaking in public is what we anticipate in our heads. I am not a psychologist or counselor, but I am a speaker and I've been in your shoes. Maybe you were traumatized about public speaking from the first day of school. Do you remember "show and tell" in school? Some of us have nightmares from those classroom experiences and some of us delighted in the opportunity to entertain a live audience. If your teacher allowed your classmates to "boo" you off the classroom floor, shame on them – they were a jerk and should not have pursued teaching children as a career. You are better than that. I really mean it.

I was in kindergarten and during our "show and tell" period our teacher asked us to bring a story from Mother Goose to share with the class because we'd be organizing the end of the year class play. Everyone came with their stories: Old Mother Hubbard and her doggy and bone, The Cow Jumped Over the Moon, Humpty Dumpty, and Jack and Jill. Then it was my turn to stand up front and share about my nursery rhyme that I selected to perform for this play. I stood dumbfound at first and the teacher urged, "Lisa do you have a story to share?" I shook my head no. She asked as cheerfully and encouragingly as possible and suggested, "Would you like to be Mother Goose?" to which I replied, "No, I don't want to be a goose! I want to be a nurse." Shocked, the teacher smiled and said, "A nurse? There is no nurse in the Mother Goose Nursery Rhymes." I pointed out, "OK, but when Jack and Jill go down the hill they come tumbling down and I could put a band-aid on their knees." The kids laughed, the teacher chuckled and then she agreed we could improvise and add a "nurse" part to the play. So I was elected to Emcee. I announced the welcome to the play, recited the Jack and Jill story, applied the band-aids and thanked everyone at the end. See how we get our start in public speaking from show and tell?

The queasy feeling we experience at the idea of speaking in front of "someone" is totally linked into what we believe about ourselves. We have a belief that audiences are bad for us, but it's really about what we think of ourselves on the inside. What we think about ourselves and those around us is what we bring forth in our reality. Stop second-guessing yourself. You were made for the moment when you step on stage and speak the words you are gifted to speak.

You drive in traffic? You can handle people. You shop in a mall? Crowds are not an issue. Have you gone to a play or concert? Fans are cool. Do you eat in a restaurant? Noise and confusion are second nature to you. You got this. Don't over complicate things.

3.2 Study Your Audience

If you were here in front of me, I'd tell you face to face you are better than any negative audience experience you have experienced. Unfortunately, in school, business, family, and life we eat our young, we destroy our youth, and we snuff out creativity. What are we thinking? We live in a world of human faults, depravity and selfishness. Allow me to edify you as you read this today and affirm that you have something important, creative, intelligent, useful, clever, significant, funny, motivational and inspirational to say. May I be your first fan?

Write about it: When you think of an audience, what is your mental image? What are you anticipating or expecting?

Exercise: LOOK around at the faces of people in the next audience of which you are a member. Note that some smile, some nod, some stare, some looked glazed over, some snore but none have attacked a speaker! Now study yourself as an audience member. How do you act and respond to a speaker? Have you ever noticed your own face while listening to someone speak? Have you personally attacked any speakers yet?

Make it a habit to study each audience you join in the next week. They really are not pit vipers waiting to strike. They are more like a group of golden retrievers, sitting, staying, watching, adoring your every word, and nodding every now and then.

I remember speaking to a group of "elderly" women at an event. I was energized and enthused to share the message and I saw people nodding and smiling throughout the talk. At the end of the event, I thanked the women and shook hands. One woman with hearing aids in both ears arrived in line and this woman pulled my hand toward her as she leaned in and shrieked, "Honey, you were really, really, good. Inspirational message, but we couldn't hear you in the back of the room because the two women in front of us were snoring." I guess my best audiences don't actually HEAR me... they are sleeping and snoring!

Here's another secret: *yawning* is not about you, it is about the person in the audience who is sleepy from being up all night with a screaming baby, or a person distracted by his own stress and complications in life. These are things you as a speaker cannot control or prevent.

Here is the beginning of the secret for the cure of audience phobia: the audience is what we expect them to be. Next time you have to speak, imagine your audience as groups of harmless, fluffy, sweet bunnies sitting transfixed on your talk. Alternatively, imagine them as a showroom filled with high-end sports cars? How about a group of kind, endearing people who are just excited to see you and can't wait to hear what you have to say? Does it comfort you to know you could have a sleeping audience? If so, go with that mental image. Whatever it takes. Speak to the sleeping; what harm can there be in that? Do any of those images work for you? Focus on a mental picture of whatever works to soothe you.

Write about it: What mental image of an audience would soothe you the most?

_____

_____

_____

_____

_____

_____

_____

_____

Whom do you want to impact with what you say? Think about your ideal audience: moms, retirees, nurses, teachers, professionals, athletes, sales people, youth, men, women, church, politics, the employed and unemployed.

Write about it: Describe your ideal audience.

_____

_____

_____

What will your audience take home from your event? Will there be a handout, goody bag, token of remembrance, certificate, bookmark, coffee mug, or other physical item?

In my workshops, I like to provide 20% teaching time, but 80% of the time I want workshop participants in the front of the room communicating, speaking, and talking to their fellow participants. Want to learn to swim? We have to get in the water. My conferees stand up front repeatedly until they like it. When I work with people one-on-one, they spend 95% time speaking and 5% receiving positive feedback about their experience. I know it seems inhumane to make a student speaker get up front and speak, but my purpose is to aid you in getting up there even if I lose some friends for the short term. In the end, people thank me. This works because in my workshops we edify the speaker; we hold the speaker up and build confidence. Together we shatter negative beliefs and move you positively into the speaker you were created to be. It really works. Adrenaline is going to flow, so use it to fuel what you say. Stop hyperventilating. Pour out your energy to others. You're doing *great*.

Ancient Authentic Advice
Amazement gripped the audience,
and they began to discuss what had happened.
"What sort of new teaching is this?" they asked excitedly.
"It has such authority!"

Phase 4.0 –
The Revision of Rejection
Mastering Feedback for Movement, Motivation & Magnification

I want to discuss the topic of rejection. First, be prepared for other people's opinions. Everyone has one and most times people will speak before they think and they will provide feedback prior to you asking for it. Not everyone speaks confidence into another's life. Now, when you do ask for feedback, be prepared for what you receive: some of it might touch on sensitive nerves.

Rejection is the act of refusing to agree with something, refusing to believe in something, or refusing to make use of something. We might reject something because it is not good enough or not the right thing or it doesn't meet a required standard or is otherwise unsuitable. That is the technical definition of rejection. Rejection is a transitive verb an action word.

But here's where we get all messed up. Rejection is more about the rejecter then the rejected. As the rejected, we can choose how to deal with rejection. We can magnify the negative feedback into something that potentially destroys us, or we can reject the rejection. How do you reject rejection? Take the unkind and unfriendly experience, say to yourself, "NEXT," and then choose to move forward.

I have a theory on rejection because I have spent too much of my adult life feeling less than valuable in many circumstances. Allow me to share a story. I was attending a writer's conference a short time prior to the birth of this book and at that event I felt horrified, traumatized, and humiliated. I felt rejected. Why, you might ask? Well, let me explain. I had scheduled a one-on-one session with a writing critic for feedback on a proposal I had written for a fiction work. I was super excited about and confident in my proposal. I meet with the man and yes, I was a little nervous but I knew my fabulous "pitch" would overshadow any misspellings or grammatical errors on my written manuscript. We exchanged pleasantries and he says, "I'd like to read your manuscript first." The hair on the back of my neck is already standing up because he didn't follow my plan for his critique. (Just for the record, I hate the word critique.)

His eyes glance over the first two sentences and he pauses and takes out a **pen**. I am thinking to myself, "He wouldn't *dare* make a mark on my precious manuscript" as he scribbles a huge question mark in the right hand corner. Without looking up, he muses, "Is this in first person or third person narrative?" I gulped and spoke to the top of his downcast head, "I think it is in first person." He responds, "No, you switched persons." I stayed quiet. He continues for two more lines and marks my manuscript again while saying, "This needs to be indented, it is clearly a new paragraph" and drawing the paragraph indention "P" symbol. I flashed back to fourth grade writing class and some nightmare jostled into my cranium. I feel my face flush (and for those of you who know me, I am not a blusher) and at this point I am beginning to fume on the inside. He continues his review of my document, jotting notes, adding commas, circling misspellings, and editing everything in sight. You get the point, right?

Rejection! He did not state "*I hate your work!*" but this was the message I was receiving. Rejection was the emotion I experienced in response to what *I asked him to do*. I made an appointment for this. Some people actually pay for these critiques. His intention was not to minimize me as a writer but to complete a task I had volunteered my work for. Now I had a choice about how to react. I wish I could say that I accepted his feedback gracefully and then decided it was simply someone's opinion that may or may not be helpful. Nope, I did the complete opposite in all my maturity and wisdom. I promptly stood up managed to thank him and shake his hand. Then I rushed back to my hotel room, put on my pajamas and got in bed. This was 4:30 in the afternoon. I decided I would just go home the next day and end my suffering. I was tired, I was ferklempt, and I was done. I figured that if I could pout myself to sleep by 5:00 p.m. then I would sleep through the night and get to the morning more quickly so I could be on my way. No such luck. I had a roommate whom I was responsible to drive back to the airport for her flight back home and couldn't abandon her in my pity party.

Around 6 p.m. she walks into the hotel room, is surprised to see me in my bed, and says, "Lisa, are you OK?" I looked at her with red swollen eyes and muttered, "This is not for me, and I am going home." She replied, "What happened?" I dramatically performed and reenacted every word, move and experience I had with this man with whom I chose to have a feedback session. She commiserated with me, saying, "I had some bad experiences too." There is something wonderful about friends that just know how to lift you out of the quagmire we lodge ourselves into, isn't there? Long story short, she coerced me to get dressed and go to dinner and we had a cathartic time of venting about our experiences that day.

The next day, I am still feeling the rush of negative emotions every time I see the manuscript reviewer. I hiss some not-so-nice thoughts to myself and begin planning my escape from the conference. I decide to eat lunch before departing and I am walking toward the chow house of the retreat center when I run into two women. I was not in the mood to talk to anyone (which is not my norm, since I speak for a living) but I summoned up my best "Hello" to the women and they responded by starting a conversation. They asked about my profession, to which I replied, "I am a voice-over artist." I couldn't bear to admit I had ever written anything. They inquired about that line of work, and then I ask the first question back. "What do you all do?" Lynellen responded first, saying she was a publisher with a small Christian press in Virginia. Then Elizabeth told me she was a professor but also a novelist working on her first book and it had been a challenge. The word "CHALLENGE" lit up in neon letters in my mind. We decided to eat lunch together and from that impromptu meeting, or divine appointment, I met my publisher for the book you hold in your hands today. The original fiction work I had the critique experience with moved me to what was really supposed to be my first written work.

4.1 Moving Forward After Rejection

My point is that rejection can move us to a different place, and it might even be a *positive* place instead of a negative place. The powerful feeling of rejection can change the trajectory of where we thought we were going to where we wind up landing instead. In sales jobs, professional salespeople will tell you it takes 10 "No" responses to get to one "Yes." Sales professionals learn to cope with the "No" responses by reminding themselves not to view the "No" as a rejection but to simply move to the NEXT person and see if they want what they are offering to sell. Please do not allow rejection to stifle you as a person, artist, writer, or speaker. Let it MOVE you to a new place. In many cases, the new place will be the place you were supposed to be from the beginning. Rejection refines us and redirects us to what's next.

Ancient Authentic Advice
Your words stand fast and true;
Rejection doesn't faze you.

Phase 5.0 – Self Strengths
Personality Practicum

If you know your speaking personality, you'll know your limits and strengths. I classify my personality type as an extroverted introvert. I encourage you to find out what your personality type is because it will aid you in discovering your speaking style and comfort level.

Exercise: There are several websites where you can take a free personality test. Use a search engine to find results for the phrase "free personality type test." Spend a few hours online taking several different personality tests such as the Myers-Briggs and the DISC personality test.

Write about it: What did you learn about your personality type?

Write about it: How do you define YOU? Circle each word that appeals to you, then write any other meaningful words.

Encourager	Motivator	Inspirer
Cheerleader	Professor	Artist
Helper	Supporter	Activist
Nurturer	Leader	Thinker
Poet	Performer	Communicator
Promoter	Educator	Trainer
Instructor	Student	Coach
Dreamer	Catalyst	Facilitator
Sparkler	Director	Actor
Comedian	Leader	Frontrunner
Trailblazer	Spearhead	Organizer
Manager	Guide	Mentor
Advisor	Guru	Counselor
World Changer	Advocate	Superstar
Chief	Planner	Executive
Commander	Believer	Orator

Other meaningful words: _____

_____

_____

_____

5.1 Descriptive Self Statement

Use the top three words you chose to describe yourself, and fill in the sentence below. Here is an example: Lisa Heidrich is a Communicator, Coach, and Catalyst. Now it's your turn:

_____(your name) is a _____,

_____, _____.

Your speaking personality does not always mirror your *personality*-personality. Honestly, some of the best and most powerful speakers are introverts *and* extroverts. There are no preferences or limitations either way. Knowing your style and comfort zone is one key to moving from whispering to speaking aloud.

Write about it: How would you describe yourself as a speaker? Circle all that apply, then write any other meaningful words.

Scared	Nervous	Interested
Dramatic	Philosophical	Comedic
Fast speaker	Slow speaker	Educational
Motivational	Chatty	Articulate
Conversational	Eloquent	Formal
Gossipy	Inarticulate	Incoherent
Informal	Lyrical	Pithy
Rambling	Rhetorical	Succinct
Verbose		

Other words and thoughts:

Write about it: Does your current style of speaking suit you? Why or why not?

_____

_____

_____

_____

_____

_____

_____

_____

    For now, I'd ask that you pause any mental tapes of negative thinking and open your mind and heart to the possibility of speaking confidence. How you speak reflects your personality. *What* you speak about (or *why* you speak) reflects your passions. Our personalities and our passions are often intertwined.

5.2 Descriptive Passion Statement

    What would you do day after day, saying you cannot wait to get up to do it, and would do it for *free*? When you figure that out, you've found your passion. When you find your passion, you know what your speaking platform is. When you have those two things in front of you then you can speak about it to anyone within earshot. Shout it out so the world can hear you. Speak with confidence. You can do it if you want to.

    If we look back into our memories, we can discover what our passions are. What you loved as a kid is most likely similar to what you love today. For me that is speaking and elocution edification.

Write about it: What were your interests as a child? What are your interests today?

Ask yourself this question and chew on it for a bit: "What makes my belly burn or my heart ache?"

What is your *passion statement*? To construct your passion statement you will need to select a few words from the previous exercises. What were your defining words? List some of them here. Here is an example of the words I would choose: *educator, motivator, and world changer.*

How would you formulate these words together to establish and convey your PASSION statement? Think "your brand." You might construct something like this as a passion statement: "Educating the Youth on Social Justice Issues to Change, Innovate, and Inspire the World's Future permanently."

Then shorten it: "Educating Youth to Innovate and Inspire the Future."

Even shorter: "Educating Youth, Inspiring Futures." Alternatively, "Youth Educator, Future Innovator."

See how passion statements develop? Maybe your book is about this topic, maybe your life has exemplified this theme, perhaps you have just felt the urging and calling to speak up for a cause. However you are stirred is what your passion statement will represent to others. From your passion statement, you will have a starting point for speaking engagements, workshops, advertisements, and websites and wherever else you want the world to know about who you are and how you want to influence your audience.

Keep a few notes as you process through this pivotal question. As ideas pop into your mind, jot them down and ask others for their opinion of who they think you are. It is a journey and there is no rush.

Ancient Authentic Advice
For where your treasure is, there your heart will be also.

Phase 6.0 – Figuratively Speaking
Words Make or Break Us

Words can make or break us, can't they? I know I have experienced times in life where one word lifted me out of a pit of despair or where one word sank me in a quagmire. They can be simple words like "YES" and "NO." Think on that a bit. They are mighty "one worders." How does "TERRIFIC" sound? Or "BRILLIANT"? Now how about "RIDICULOUS"? Keep in mind that when you tell your story, the power of a single word is critical. You don't need numerous words, just key words. Before we get started, make sure you have a Thesaurus — any kind, digital or bound in old-fashioned ink and paper. Just make sure you have one and promise me you will use it!

Exercise: Use your thesaurus to write a short, inspiring message. Maybe take a meaningful Bible verse and rewrite it. Or a quote or poem. Call four people and leave them your custom message on their voice mail. Do this three times this week. That gives you 12 opportunities to practice speaking and brighten someone's day too.

6.1 The Power of Double Entendre

Let's move into figures of speech and one of my favorite ways to share with others: double entendre. A double entendre is a phrase that can have two meanings. The first meaning is usually obvious and straightforward, but the second meaning may be a bit more obscure and is often ironic, sarcastic, or risqué. There is something about irony, sarcasm, and tongue-in-cheek that resonates inside us. I love double entendre because it delivers more than one message, and makes your listener think and remember you as a speaker. We want our audiences to THINK so they are looking less AT us and listening more intently TO us. Mostly, we'd like them to remember something about what we said. Does that idea stir you?

An example of a double entendre is the title of this book. Did you notice it? *Speaking Confidence.*

The first meaning is obvious: We want to have confidence speaking in front of our audience.

The double entendre is more subtle: We want to speak confidence into our audience.

Write about it: Develop a double entendre for your talk. See how creative you can be, then practice saying it to yourself. How does it sound? Try it out on another person... yes, speak it aloud. Write your double entendre here. What reaction did it receive when you shared it with another person?

_____

_____

_____

_____

_____

_____

_____

6.2 Oxymorons and Acrostics

A second type of figurative speech is the oxymoron. An oxymoron combines opposite or contradictory words together for special effect. For example, 'jumbo shrimp', 'smart idiot', 'almost ready', 'adult children', and 'awfully pretty'. The point of an oxymoron is to create a new image in the mind of the listener, to get them to think about the contradiction. Oxymora (the plural of oxymoron) can also be used to add humor to your speech. Humor can make your point more memorable.

The third type of word game I enjoy is creating acrostics. An acrostic is a type of poem, but you definitely don't have to rhyme in an acrostic. An acrostic is simply a series of lines where the first letter of each line is chosen because those letters also form a name or a word. An acrostic helps get a point across and leaves a memorable idea with your audience. It also eliminates copious notes for a speaker to remember because each letter in the acrostic will "cue" the speaker as to the next topic. Here is an example of one acrostic I might use to convey my point to my audience: S.P.E.A.K.

Smile

Presenting

Enthusiastically

Authentic

Kindness

When I conduct a speaking workshop, this acrostic is how I arrange my teaching topics. The participants remember the letters S.P.E.A.K., the word associated with each letter, and the instruction related to each letter in the acrostic. When we S.P.E.A.K. we must first, **S**mile (engage the audience, calm our nerves) then we begin **P**resenting our information, topic, or message. We smile and present **E**nthusiastically. Otherwise, stay home. If we are not enthusiastic about our work, why speak about it? Your message is important so deliver it with conviction. Also note: enthusiasm is *contagious*. Its root word is *"en theos"* or *with God*, so when you have God going with you, there is no way to be less than exhilarated. As you observe other speakers, are they hum drum and boring or are they zealous? I bet you'll remember those who were enthusiastic. Being Authentic is what every audience wants from their presenter: real life, real stories. Be genuine in your presentation. Don't be someone you're not; just be the best you that you can be. Finally, we S.P.E.A.K. in and with **K**indness. We open and close our talk being grateful to the audience. Thank your audience before and after you speak; this is professional speaking protocol. We leave them with an inspiration or appreciative word to take home.

See how acrostics work? An acrostic generates fewer notes, is a great bullet point reminder that identifies our purpose, and gives strength to what we say or SPEAK.

Write about it: Design an acrostic that you might use as bullet points for your material. If you desire, you can use the one I listed in this chapter, but use your own defining words for each letter in the S.P.E.A.K. acrostic. Write your acrostic here:

6.3 Creative Chutzpah

Determine what figures of speech you might use to make your talk more interesting, humorous, real, and memorable. Let the crowd know you have chutzpah and show your confidence like the word game hero you were created to be. The figures of speech and elocution you combine into your final presentation are keys to your vocal performance. It's just a matter of words practiced and spoken aloud. Be creative.

Ancient Authentic Advice
Make a careful exploration of who you are and the work you have been given, and then sink yourself into that. Don't be impressed with yourself. Don't compare yourself with others. Each of you must take responsibility for doing the creative best you can with your own life.

Phase 7.0 –
Transformative Narrative
The Art of Storytelling

There is nothing like a good story. We all remember favorite stories we heard as kids. Some are basic childhood stories; some might even be family stories. Everyone can gain from learning how to tell a good story. Most successful entrepreneurs have mastered the art of storytelling. It links to sales success, as well as personal success. Once you are able to captivate someone's attention with a story, you can persuade him or her to agree with what you are trying to present to them. Transformative narrative is truly the ART of Story Telling.

Storytelling is a timeless tradition that dates back before the written word. People would memorize folklore and stories full of lessons, consequences, humor and morals that have shaped our culture for generations. With the influx of electronic communication tools, the idea of talking and telling stories is *diminishing*. However, everyone loves to hear a good story. We are wired for communicating through anecdotes that teach life lessons and warnings. I am sad that storytelling is becoming a lost art in many businesses, schools, families, and social gatherings.

Nowadays, we are more likely to plug a child into visual media instead of sitting down and teaching them to listen to a story while someone speaks. I remember when kids had to sit with their parents for the whole sermon on Sunday. Talk about temperament training. In some churches now, we transport kids to other rooms during the sermon so they are entertained with their peers. Do we do them an injustice by that type of segregation? Maybe. I remember wishing on many Sundays that my kids had heard the same sermon I heard.

Have we become lazy as a society by relying on computer applications and power point slides to convey what we desire to say? Captivating stories can really make us great speakers. So how do we learn to become good storytellers?

7.1 Timeless Memories

Stories create memories. Do you remember a tradition in your home? Maybe your birthday, or a holiday like Thanksgiving or Christmas, for example. Is there a story you remember being told on that holiday repeatedly? I do. Every birthday, I remind my sons of the story of their birth. What happened that day, what the nurses said about them being so cute, how they screamed as a baby and how excited I was to have them as my boys. They know the stories by heart and don't always want me to share them around certain company (i.e., a potential girlfriend or a man-buddy) for fear of embarrassment. But the truth is people love stories. It is a way to learn about someone and remember something special. Stories bring to life an experience that you never want to fade away. This leads me to the next point.

Stories are timeless and can go to places we never imagined. It is exciting to witness someone else telling your story to another person. Retelling the story indicates that you were successful in sharing the message that was on your heart. For example, stories involving history, Biblical truths, bibliographies, awkward situations, and funny moments all travel to places we never dreamed they would go. How many times have you heard the story of Noah's Ark? Two by two, Noah collected all the animals to save them from the flood. It starts out as a dramatic event ending with some lessons we might still find thought provoking today. Like, how did the animals and people all multiply to produce the nations we have now?

That makes for a good story which keeps others thinking and talking about it.

My grandmother used to tell my sister and me this story of my mom when she was a little girl. They would go walking, my mom in a vintage stroller and my grandmother pushing her baby and buggy down the streets of their neighborhood. As they would walk my grandmother would give my mom snacks, little toys, etc., to keep her entertained and in the carriage. One day my grandmother gave my mom raisins to nibble while she was browsing through a shop. As my mom asked for more raisins my grandmother would gladly oblige.

The conversation went like this. My grandmother would act out pushing the carriage and then act out my mom sitting in her carriage and my mom's antics in reaching up her little hand and holding it out saying, "Puweese Mommy more radins." My sister and I would laugh at my grandmother's impersonation of my mom as a little kid.

The story continues that they shopped all day and ate raisins *all day*. When they got home, my mom said to her mommy, "My nose hurts and something is in it." My grandmother now would demonstrate how she looked into my mom's nose, checked her forehead for fever and tried to reassure her daughter everything was just fine. Then my grandmother would get super dramatic and say, "ALL OF A SUDDEN your mom says to me, 'Mommy I gonna swweeze... Ahhh... ahhhh... ahhh Chooooooo!'" My grandmother would demonstrate this HUMONGOUS SNEEZE and explain how 50,000 raisins splattered and sprayed all over the place. Grandmother said to my mom, "WHAT did you do with the raisins?" To which my mom replied, "I put da radins in my nose."

My grandma would laugh, we would laugh and the story ended. I used to wonder why would my mom do such a thing. Now

I realize she was just a child. But hearing the story as a little girl myself made me feel a connection with my mom by knowing she was once young and mischievous too. That is the timeless beauty of the art of storytelling. It goes on and on and travels to places we never expect. Make your story compelling and informative. Share a meaningful message. A memorable story is not easily forgotten.

7.2 Create & Tell Your Story

Compare storytelling to a stand-up comedian. A good storyteller will include comedy to keep the audience's attention. Take an everyday experience that you find funny and thought provoking make it into a story. Include your own dramatic effects and facts or ideas. Open with the three points you want to leave with your audience and close by repeating the three points. Make them a catchy three points.

For example, in my mom's raisin story the three catchy points I might open up with would be:

1.   Never Push a Baby Carriage ALL day long
2.   Watch Where your Raisins Go
3.   Being a Mom Takes Bravery

Get the idea? Be brief and not overly detailed. Use gestures and body language to share your message. Use timing and pauses so the audience has a chance to "get it" and laugh a little. Most storytellers and comics are not people with extraordinary lifestyles; they have just mastered the art of storytelling.

Write about it: Recall a family story that has influenced your life in some way. What did you glean from it? What was funny about it? What type audience could you share that story with?

Exercise: Create a story you'd like to tell. Arrange it with graphics or simple drawings and then speak it to someone.

Write about it: How did your story turn out? How did your audience react?

Exercise: My mom's raisin story might be perfect for a speech at a Mommy group of some kind. A good story can be applicable to multiple audiences with the right spin on it. Who else could the raisin story be shared with?

_____

_____

_____

Write about it: Spin the story you created above and list different target audiences it would work for:

_____

_____

_____

_____

_____

_____

_____

Great stories incite us to action. My response to my grandmother's raisin story was to swear, "I will never eat raisins again!!" That story also taught me a lesson as mom: watch what your kids do with snacks you give them! How I enjoy reminding my mom of what she did as a little girl. I find myself chuckling to know a nose stuffing raisin lover raised me. Moreover, yes, she still loves raisins and gets great delight in harassing me by putting raisins into everything she cooks.

What story do you remember that incites you to action? A story can be on any subject and usually includes a funny part, a lesson, an informative part, a recall back to history and then a message that propels us forward in our thinking and daily lives. Arm your audience with a good interactive story. It does not have to be perfect.

Exercise: Record a transformative narrative—something you read or heard-- that changed your life. Share the recording with someone and ask for feedback on your performance.

Write about it: Why was your narrative powerful to you? What reaction did your audience have to your recording?

Storytelling is magical and inspires us. Talking with people inspires us and leads us to action. When we hear a great speaker share a heartfelt story it changes us. The power of our voice is like no other strength. The jaw of a donkey can kill a million men. That is figurative, of course, and no one in his or her right mind is going to war with a jackass jaw. But, oh, the power in saying something stupid or hurtful, right? The tongue is a two edged sword with the power to bring life or to destroy. It does take creativity and brainpower to develop a story and master the skill of storytelling but, in the end, it is well worth the effort. Who knows how many generations you might inspire to action by a well-told story?

7.3 Keys of Storytelling

Not all stories that we share will be funny and light-hearted. Sad stories can have a huge impact on our audience too, but they can also be difficult for you if they cause you to experience emotion that negatively affects your speaking voice. If you decide to tell an emotional, passionate anecdote, keep a tissue or hanky available in case you need it. I have learned many times that when expressing a sensitive story my nose runs and my eyes leak. Wiping your nose and eyes with the printout of your talk is NOT recommended! I have cautioned you in advance. No one wants to shake your hand after a snotty recounting of your life crisis, renovation, revolution or trans-formation. Ladies, wear waterproof mascara and eye makeup or look like a raccoon (*in public!*). Try the mascara prior to using it in case of any allergy.

Exercise: Practice getting emotionally involved today. Get mushy, let your voice squeak, say something difficult to someone. Recite a poem or something that digs up intense reactions and makes you feel raw. I know it is uncomfortable, but do it anyway. Now as you whimper with your words, practice breathing and restart your recita-tion. Begin to train yourself to breathe and share the intense mo-ment. When this type of moment happens, you will have to believe and trust in the training to recover in public.

Exercise: Leave a motivating voice message for someone special to you. Be mushy and gushy. Tell them one thing you like best about them. THANK them for being your friend, spouse, sister, child, etc. For example: "Hey Pam, thanks for being a great listener. I always know I can be comforted by your power in listening. You are a spe-cial and loved friend."

Exercise: What do you want to say to someone special for them to remember during their lifetime? Tell them now. The sooner the better.

Key things to remember in the art of storytelling:
1. Be brief. Arrange your story by typing it out, drawing it out, or outlining on note cards.
2. Share details.
3. Give the story twists and turns in the action.
4. Work the crowd and engage with your audience. Include something emotional, whether it's happiness or sadness.
5. Act out characters with various gestures and voices.
6. Practice. Tell your story in front of a mirror or video so you see how it sounds and looks.
7. Reiterate the points of the story.
8. End on a laugh or with a provoking thought.
9. Thank your audience.

Not everyone prefers to tell a story; this is very individualized and has to be something from your heart. It's OK to never do it. You have a choice. However, as you go about your day this week look for the stories in life as they are unfolding. This is the best way to get your "mojo convo" working for you. What is a mojo convo? Is is a heart / passion / magnetic / real–life-story that touched you and brought you to your place of "mojo" (slang for magnetic quality trait that attracts or charms others). "Convo" is my shortcut for conversation. Combining the two words becomes a Lisa Word I refer to as your "mojo convo." Some people are natural at sharing a story but many need guidance and training to prefect this skill and technique. Think about it, ponder it a bit, and feel absolutely no pressure to have to ever do it. This is completely optional.

Write about it: What happened today that moved you, gave you goose bumps or became something that stirred your heart and soul and you cannot erase from your mind? If you have a moment like this, you have found a potential "mojo convo." Write about it here.

Ancient, Authentic Advice
A long storytelling afternoon.
His storytelling fulfilled prophecy;
I will open my mouth and tell stories;
I will bring out into the open
things hidden since the world's first day.

Phase 8.0 – Vocal Performance
Quality Elocution and Articulation

Articulation is the act of presenting clear speech, enunciation or joining something together. When we articulate we say things the absolute BEST way we can. Pronunciation, grammar, style, and tone are key speaking settings. Accents are interesting, timing is important, and volume can be controlled. Your elocution matters. Elocution is your personal oral delivery, how you speak, your timing, animation in your voice, and body language. Elocution is your unique and creative speaking performance.

I began my career as an elocution editor way back in my pre-teens when my sister began competing in elocution contests. I was her audience and coach, at times listening to her diction repeatedly until she had her pontification perfect. She also gave me my start as a voice-over artist by reading to her the same books endlessly, until we discovered taping the stories could satisfy her desire to hear her favorite stories repeatedly.

Have you determined your style yet? Speaking style, or elocution, will mirror your lifestyle, training or culture. We are all diverse from vocal cord to vocal cord. We dress a certain way, have our hair a certain way, decorate our lives a certain way, and we speak a certain way. Accents, pronunciation, inflection, and tone all affect the way you say something. When you talk with someone, do you look into their eyes and speak at them or to them? There IS a difference.

One-on-one conversations aren't my strength. I'd rather send a sweet card or note for intimate words. I prefer one-to-100. That is actually easier for me and better represents my speaking style. Give me a crowd. However, my one-on-one speaking engagements are sometimes more important than any arena or crowd venue. When

I speak to my sons, it is important to engage that moment. When I visit a friend who is upset or scared, that is a sensitive one-on-one appointment. You get the idea. Some of you might be saying, "Now she's talking. I can do the one-on-one; it's the bigger venues that take my breath away."

Similar to exercising, singing, playing an instrument, cooking, or writing, practicing speaking develops our speaking. Exercise your voice, even just for a few minutes a day. This can be accomplished by singing, talking with someone, or talking to yourself. Go visit someone you haven't seen in a long time. Visit a nursing home. Go interview someone. Get a voice recorder and tape yourself reading the paper, a book, a greeting card or your latest manuscript. Grab your e-book, the dictionary, or a blog and read aloud to yourself. Listen to your voice. It is beautiful. This is the season to share, develop, and use your voice. Give it a shot or *another shot*. Just like muscles, your voice will get stronger as you use it. Get used to your voice and be willing to share your secrets with others. Don't be selfish and keep your voice to yourself.

8.1 Word Games

I adore word games. Scrabble, Boggle, Words With Friends, Word Searches, and Word Scrambles. I admit I am a word junkie. Words just work for me. There is nothing better than a twenty-five cent word like 'cacophony.' I bet those twenty-five cent dazzlers excite you as well. Especially those of you who are authors — words are your bag. For me it's cathartic to jot down ideas, devotions, thoughts and stories. My mind goes faster than my fingers could ever type. I have to speak to think, so writing is just a result of all the thoughts in my mind that need purging so my brain has some room to relax. Word games are excellent exercises for the brain. As a speaker, you should routinely exercise your mental dictionary and thesaurus by playing word games and by journaling.

Exercise: Play a game of Scrabble, or complete a word search or crossword puzzle. Exercise your mind with words today.

Write about it: What are your favorite word games?

8.2 Sound Bites = Listening

I like hearing Morgan Freeman or Patrick Stewart speak. They can render any message and I am *listening*. Morgan Freeman's voice sets an atmosphere of wisdom, trust, and comfort. I think he has a soothing and melodious voice. Patrick Stewart (a.k.a. Captain Jean-Luc Picard) has a handsome English accent that makes even the worst news sound delicious and interesting. LISTEN to someone you admire. Identify their elocution. That is what grabs you.

Exercise: Call a friend you have not spoken to in awhile. Call your Mom. Call your kids. Listen to your voice and theirs. We don't take time to really listen to how we sound and how others sound. Turn on the radio and listen to voice of a disc jockey, singer, or news reporter.

Write about it: Is there a speaker you admire or wish you sounded like? Can you figure out why?

_____

_____

_____

_____

Write about it: If you could mail order your vocal sound what would it be like?

_____

_____

_____

_____

Write about it: Change your voice mail message today. Listen to your voice, it is wonderful! Record a new message repeatedly for the next 2 days. Listen to yourself. How does your voice and message change as you record it over and over?

_____

_____

_____

_____

The average person speaks about 100 words a minute, but a fast talker can utter up to 140 words per minute. A typist with decent speed types an average of 60 words a minute. A court reporter can take down dictation as quickly as 200 words per minute. The average woman speaks around 30,000 words a day while the average male might only speak around 7,000 words a day. No wonder there is an ongoing battle of the sexes. Who is really speaking and who is really listening? Our speed of speech is important in conveying our message. We want it to be memorable.

8.3 Selah, Practice & Punctuate

Listening to yourself and practicing are critical for all speaking. In this chapter, I am including a devotion I wrote. It has practical information to motivate you to seek out your gifts and natural talents, but mostly I have included it for you to read ALOUD. Yes, read it aloud with feeling, inflection, and intonation. Be as dramatic as you like, and deliver it in a professorial way. Try a few different styles. Act like a news anchor and deliver it like the headline news. Give it a dramatic touch as if you were in an Elizabethan play. Read it with a foreign accent. Call someone and read it to them.   Go ahead. I'll wait right here for you. READ ALOUD, please.

THE GIFT YOU WERE MADE TO BRING

You can't fit a square peg into a round hole...if I've heard that once, I've heard it a thousand times.
Truth is — it is true.
Oh yeah — you can force it in or reshape that square into a roundish fit but does that really work?
Not really — and what does it say about how we are created uniquely in the image of God?
I have always considered myself the type of person who sought out the gifts and talents in others.
As a speaker coach, nursing administrator and as a women's ministry divisional director, connecting the right person with their natural gift set is vital for reaching optimum satisfaction in both the workplace and in ministry opportunities. It is important to me to learn others' gifts and talents to help them work harmoniously in the Body of Christ. It is the way God ordered it — so why not take the Master's lead? For lists of spiritual gifts, check out Romans 12:6-8 and 1 Corinthians 12:1-11 (verse 4: Now there are diversities of gifts, but the same Spirit) and Ephesians 4:11-13 (He gave some, apostles; and some,

prophets; and some, evangelists; and some, pastors and teachers). These verses are great reminders that God planned the perfecting of us regular people for the work of His ministry, and most of all for the edification of the body of Christ. Over my professional years, I have had great success and satisfaction in working with others to determine their gifts and talents and then plugging them into various areas to use those gifts to glorify God. Discovering spiritual gifts is a great way to get to know your friends and loved ones!

Google "spirituals gifts" for a myriad of tools that will be helpful to you. Here are two resources I recommend: Life Keys: Discover Who You Are, by Jane A.G. Kise, David Stark, and Sandra Krebs Hirsch. Second, the online Ephesians 4 Ministry survey tool identifies spiritual gifts especially for team-focused ministry at: http://store.churchgrowth.org/epages/ChurchGrowth.sf

You know when the wise men went to visit the babe in the manger, they each brought gifts. Each Magus was unique in what he offered baby Jesus. What gift do you bring to God? I learned in a retreat years ago that if we can think back to our childhood and determine what we loved to do, that is where we'd find our natural God-given talent. My youngest son, Chris, loved to cook as a kid and now he is a fantastic Chef with a national restaurant chain. Matthew, my oldest, was always the peacemaker and is working toward his degree as a counselor. Another example is my friend who is an artist: as a kid, color and paint induced all day excitement. Today my friend is painting full time as unto the Lord, and utilizing God's gifts and talents while also selling each work for some nice prices!

In Colossians 3:23, God's word simply says, "work for God and not your boss" -- so work as you would if Jesus was in the supervisor's office. Having gifts and talents is part of who we are as the body of Christ. Each one of us is to fill a role and bring a unique gift to the Lord. My friend might bring God the best and most beautiful painting ... what would you bring? Be the best you can be using the gifts you were made to bring. (Written by Lisa Heidrich, all rights reserved. Portions of this "To Inspire You" devotional were publicized by Stonecroft Ministries, web publication 2012. Revisions made for book publication by the author.)

I am on the edge of my seat. How did my devotional sound coming out of your mouth? Did you make it sound interesting? How was your elocution and enunciation of the words presented in this devotion? See, you are getting this.

Exercise: Practice your elocution. Find a poem, story, joke, or song. Read it aloud and record yourself. Practice it and record it five times until the elocution electrifies you.

Write about it: What specifically did you change about your elocution that made the above exercise sound more exciting in your recording?

_____

_____

_____

_____

Be as creative as you can be in composing what you might speak one day. Write out what you will say, word by word. Place it in a binder. Key it into your favorite electronic device. Keep it handy. If your nerves get the best of you, you can simply READ your speech. See why reading aloud matters now? It is preparing you for glitches if your memory freezes. Let the MIND GAMES change to a WORD GAME. Prepare a quote or have a joke written out for an awkward moment. Have a speaker survival trick ready such as an article that supports your talk. You can take a deep breath and read it aloud. Recompose yourself. Take a drink of water, look at the letters in front of you, smile and speak. Don't worry about the pause or time it takes to collect yourself. Everyone needs a breather.

Pauses are an excellent speaking tool. Don't rush — the audience awaits you. Stay composed. Laugh aloud. Pause. Remember, it takes a little time lag for what you say to reach and connect with your audience. Our brains need a minute to process what you said. Timing is also critical when using humor. Wait seven seconds after saying something humorous. Don't be afraid of open-air moments, sometimes they are the funniest. Laugh a bit before you drop a joke; it warms up the audience to cue them *it is time to laugh.* Watch a comedian and note their timing. They giggle when they speak, and the crowd joins in.

8.4 Vocal Care & Cures

Remember to take care of your voice: it is your business asset. Here are some suggestions for remedies if your throat gets fuzzy, tired, sore, or inflamed.

- Smoke, dust, and air irritants are all antagonistic to healthy vocal cords. Resist clearing your throat, yelling, and excessive coughing, as these will actually cause more inflammation and irritation to your vocal cords.
- ALWAYS warm up your voice prior to all public speaking. Sing, talk, or hum to stimulate your voice. Don't overdo it though… just 10 minutes is usually sufficient.
- A dry throat hurts and can sound crackling and hoarse. Caffeine, alcohol, menthol, eucalyptus, antihistamines, appetite depressants, diuretics, and lemon all cause drying of the vocal cords.
- Speak in phrases, not lengthy paragraphs where you strain your voice. By speaking in phrases, you can breathe between comments and keep moisture on your money-maker.
- Hydration is important to the body and especially the vocal cords. Drink good ole water prior to speaking. It is recommended to drink half your weight in ounces of water on a daily basis. Therefore, if you weigh 120 pounds your water intake would be 60 ounces of water daily. Drink water prior to your presentations and keep a bottle of water or glass of water nearby for your talks and performances.
- Using a humidifier or steam mist will help keep vocal cords

moist when air conditioning and filtered environments such as airplanes cause unnecessary dryness.

- Pineapple juice is excellent for throats because it contains a natural anti-inflammatory. Drink pineapple juice prior to speaking for a quick throat clearer and vocal cord relaxer. Pure / local honey (a natural soother with antiseptic and anti-allergy properties), strawberry juice (which causes salivation), and olives also serve as natural throat lubricants. Slippery Elm lozenges are believed to coat and protect the throat, marsh-mellow or licorice tea and figs contain mucilage and soothe a raw and sore throat. Steamed figs with cinnamon, ginger, and nutmeg are all natural antimicrobials. So drink fig tea or eat figs warm as tolerated. You can also drink these warm teas preventively for throat protection. WARM fluids are best for your vocal cords. Ice cold drinks stiffen vocal cords.

- Avoid dairy or mucous-causing foods prior to a presentation. Be careful to also avoid any foods that cause an allergic response! Don't try new foods prior to a presentation like shellfish, nuts, strawberries or anything exotic you have not eaten before.

- Always check your breath when speaking to others, and keep a throat spray, breath freshener strips, or fast melt breath mints handy. To make your own simple breath freshener, mix 1 teaspoon of salt in 6-8 ounces of warm water. Gargling with this mixture at your highest pitch will force your vocal cords together effectively. Using this combination as a mouthwash is a great way to kill and disinfect bacteria in your mouth that causes bad breath. Grab a packet of salt from a fast food restaurant and keep a packet or two in your travel bag for emergencies, then just mix with water and you are good to go.

- Vitamins A, C, and E are also useful tools. Vitamin A helps cellular development and immune support. Take vitamin C for battling and preventing the common cold. Vitamin E is a powerful anti-oxidant that protects the immune system and aids in skin cell regeneration.

It is time. You are ready. Go articulate.

Ancient Authentic Advice

Let me tell you something: Every one of these careless words is going to come back to haunt you. There will be a time of Reckoning. Words are powerful; take them seriously. Words can be your salvation. Words can also be your damnation.

Phase 9.0 – Respiration
Whisper or Shout: Remember to Breathe

Breathing is vital when speaking or storytelling. When we get nervous, we forget to breathe deeply. When you have a rush of adrenaline, your voice may become shaky unless you take the time to breathe. As we share a moving feeling or story, our emotions can get the best of us unless we breathe. Don't apologize for feelings; let them flow through you and breathe. Expand your diaphragm and breathe. Slow your speech. Breathe again and carry on. Channel your adrenaline and emotion into a strong voice. Take a moment, gather yourself together and breathe.

Breathing is not optional. If you don't breathe, you cannot speak. That is basic anatomy 101. Remember, when you rush, ramble, tear up, or experience anxiety the best cure is to breathe and wait for 7-10 seconds before saying another word. By doing this you convert angst to calm. Train your brain. Retraining your brain takes practice, so work on it. When the situation gets tough you will revert to the training you have practiced, so trust in the process.

9.1 Relax and Re-Breathe

Remember, you have something important to say. Don't let the audience get the best of you. Relax, remind yourself you were created to share your message, breathe, count to ten and breathe again. Take a drink of water, suck on a hard candy, and say a prayer. Take a walk to burn off nervous energy, jump up and down. Breathing is important for speaking. Why are you nervous? Determine why you are freaking out, address that issue and move forward. We are not perfect and never will be perfect. No one is expecting a perfect speech. It is OK to be human. Train your brain with words of affirmation that you are going to do your best and speak your best. Tell yourself:

I CAN DO THIS,

I KNOW MY MATERIAL,

I HAVE SOMETHING TO SHARE,

I AM A GREAT SPEAKER.

What you think about you bring about. Think positive. Decide you are going to do it. Get the extra stress and energy out however you can. Give a hearty guffaw, throw a temper tantrum, run five miles. Do what you need to gain composure for your moment to speak.

9.2 Lower Your Voice

With our unique voices, we can make several different sounds. Try "hissing," for example. Refine that sound a bit and you can vocalize a delicate whisper. Let me ease you into speaking by first whispering. Want to catch someone's attention? Lower your voice instead of raising it. Secrets, promises and precious endearments are vocalized in a whisper. Our hearts and audiences remember them forever. When you whisper, you capture someone's attention.

Write about it: When was the last time you whispered? And yes, it counts if you've just whispered in your head. What did you whisper?

Exercise: Try whispering to someone today.

Write about it: What was their reaction? Did you get their attention?

Whispering uses more vocal energy than speaking. Now that you have mastered this art of soft, quiet, pitch and verbalization, give your voice a break and say something aloud. Via different airflow patterns in and out of your lungs and into your mouth, you can control how you create sounds as you speak. If your voice gets shaky, you are out of air. Match your breathing with your speaking tempo. You cannot physically speak unless you pass air into your vocal cords. Did you know that you have four vocal cords? You have two true vocal cords and two false vocal cords. These four tiny folds in your voice box are what mechanically give your voice sound and power.

Exercise: Practice breathing and relaxation techniques. Learn to deep breathe. Always carry hard candy or mints with you. Speakers need to have fresh breath, but don't deep breathe with a mint in your mouth! No gum or candy on stage. Slip it in your mouth *after* you speak.

Ancient Authentic Advice
Breathe into these dead bodies so they may live again.

Phase 10.0 – Presentation Styles
Dramatic Deliverance

Now…You've been hired as a keynote speaker for a conference. Your task is to speak for twenty minutes to inspire the audience and promote your new book. This is the opportunity you have been dreaming about or maybe it is the one that has caused nightmares. Do not panic. As you develop your speech, think of this: from your material you can cultivate three or more types of talks, workshops and performances. Creating your keynote address will be a breeze once you focus on your most comfortable speaking style. Here are a few style ideas:

One: Interview style. Scribe out 6-8 questions you'd like to be asked about your work. Someone asks you the questions, and you respond just like on talk shows—easy enough.

Two: Dramatic Performance. Is there a dramatic performance that would describe your material? It doesn't have to be elaborate but would a prop help you deliver ideas? Can storytelling help?

Three: Topical style. Coordinate a familiar idea with what you want to express. For example: For many years, I was a speaker for Women's Heart Health Month. I took a topical subject (Women's HEART Health) and linked it to a Biblical teaching of how God heals our hearts.

Four: Traditional Style. Lecture, preach, address, instruct and pontificate. You are an expert on a topic, so now is your opportunity to teach your audience.

Five: Discussion/Open Mic. Begin the conversation with the audience by explaining your topics, thoughts and ideas. Then ask for questions from your live audience. If you have friends in the audience, perhaps give them a written question in advance to help prime the pump and erase those awkward silences.

Write about it: Which of the five speaking types above are you most comfortable with?

_____

_____

_____

_____

10.1 Love Yourself & Your Story

Love yourself and your story. How long is your talk? Will you open with a famous quote or maybe play a video before you speak? Do you have a testimony to share as an aside? Should you share it? As you prepare your talk, all these things truly matter. When you present, say what you want the audience to hear (your key points), say it again, and in closing repeat it one more time. Our brains need to hear it at least three times.

How will you present your talk? Will you memorize your talk? Bring a printed copy anyway. Use Index Cards? Bring an extra set. Read from a Teleprompter? Have a written or electronic copy nearby. Read from an electronic copy such as a tablet, laptop, or smartphone? Bring a paper copy as well. Write your speech in a notebook? Bring more than one copy, and/or send an extra copy via email. Will your speech open with a video or music or a dramatic reading? Send the media in advance and also bring a copy on a USB drive or CD.

Note: Always, always, always bring multiple copies of your speech, jokes, and video. I suggest three copies and also email one to yourself or someone else travelling with you.

Ancient, Authentic Advice
Death and life are in the power of the tongue,
and they who indulge in it shall eat the fruit of it {for death or life}.

Phase 11.0 –
Articulation Amplification
Microphone Mechanics and Manners

Microphones are an essential speaking tool. Here is the GOOD news: you have complete control over the words. As for the equipment (meaning the microphone and sound system), the not-so-good news is that you typically have no control over those at all. Zip. You heard me right. Nada. With that said, this chapter will help you conquer your fears about that instrument called a microphone.

Exercise: Go to a place where there are microphones and stages (i.e., church, community center, auditorium, restaurants, YMCA, theater, bar for Karaoke night) and ask to see and try out a microphone and sound system they have available.

There are about 10 different types of microphones and if you are into technical details you can research and review microphones all day. My goal here is to expose you to the most common microphone options and get you comfortable. We are not audio engineers, so the very basics are practical for our purposes. Seriously, in my workshops I like to expose the participants to different types of microphones and have them try them aloud.

We all are familiar with a corded microphone mounted at the top of a podium. We have also all seen cordless microphones that the speaker or musician can hold or connect to a microphone stand or pole. There is the lapel microphone (or "diva mic") that clips to your clothing or curves into a fitted piece around your ear. Also of note is the lavaliere mic that is hung around the neck of the speaker. There are also big BOOM ROOM and arena microphones that pan around an area to collect sound for large venues and are operated by a set manager via a constructed arm or boom.

I want to provide you practical advice about microphones. This is important: Be prepared for anything and get used to them *all*. Everywhere you speak will have its own combination of microphone and sound system. Some work well, some don't work at all. Be ready for that too. It is just the way speaking goes, so chillax and go with it. I can almost guarantee that if you love the podium and mounted mic style, the first speaking gig you go to will have a wireless mic ready for you to wear!

My best advice: do not get emotionally attached to a certain type of microphone UNLESS you want to provide your own when you speak somewhere. That option is time consuming, and pricey, but doable. Owning your own microphone is not totally unrealistic but you will have to make several preparations in advance. Sometimes this planning works, but in my experience, most times it doesn't. Professional speakers such as disc jockeys, voice-over artists, and musicians have their own microphone they travel with. This is necessary for their line of work so if you decide to have your own microphone, the choice is totally up to you. Again, I sincerely caution you not to count on being able to use your OWN microphone each and every time you talk.

My advice is to go with whatever is there — even when you make plans in advance. Perfect example: As an animated speaker, I hate being STILL. Body language is important to me. I use my hands, I walk around, I dramatize some things I say, you get the picture. I really love to use a lavaliere or lapel microphone. One time, I was traveling and speaking to a large group in Oklahoma. I had my presentation ready, my humor rehearsed, my timing perfected, and I had at least three conversations with the sound guy and the event coordinator about the lapel mic I was going to wear. (I am starting to giggle now.) I did not get the sound guy who was supposed to "hook me up." He wasn't working that night and I was basically on my own. On the stage was a podium with a mounted microphone, and nothing else. I had a dramatic conversation in my head that went something like this: "I have planned and practiced my talk to be free to move as I speak. Now I am chained to a podium?"

When you become a world-renowned speaker, you can have every detail in place before you show up. Until then, get used to going with the flow. Always feel free to inquire ahead of time about mics if you desire, but go with no fixed expectations, and be able to speak with any combination of microphones, podiums, lighting, stages, steps, video, etc. This can become a speaking barrier if you don't acquiesce and determine you are flexible in this regard. "Go with the flow" is my best advice from a "not-so-good-at-going-with-the-flow" kind of girl.

11.1 Microphone Etiquette

Let's review a few simple rules on how to work with the equipment.

- Do not blow into the mic. This causes water to settle into the condenser and will ruin the mic.
- Do not "tap" the mic because it breaks down the wires and structure of the microphone.
- Do not get too close and leave your lip prints or lipstick, lipgloss, lip balm, etc. on the mic. You will also be absorbing germs from previous speakers.
- Do not put the mic in front of the monitors or speakers. I'm sure you've heard that horrible screeching feedback loop that deafens you and everyone in the audience when a mic is too close to the monitor.

- Do keep your mouth in front of the mic. One to two inches distance is optimum for speaking. Do not rest the mic on your face, chin, cheek, nose or neck. The absolute best sound quality is in front of your mouth. Make adjustments of mic location and height as gracefully and as quietly as possible.

- Remember to back up if you are bellowing, but hover close as your volume diminishes during your talk. You are in control of those dramatic effects but you must practice them in advance.

- If you record in a radio station or studio, a "pop-screen" is used to soften your speech especially "p", "b", "s", and "t" sounds and other popping or hissing noises we make with our lips. When recording or dictating, such as in audio books, it is important to have the same settings every time you record. Check and record microphone setting and location to replicate for continued work and even vocal sound.

- Be kind to the mics you will be meeting on your journey as a speaker. Always try to get a sound check in advance of your speech.

11.2 Microphone Varieties

There are six microphone styles I'd like to brief you on.

WALKIE TALKIE style microphone: wireless lapel, la-valiere, diva, or over-the ear, headset microphone. Proper position-ing of the over-the-ear or headset microphone is about ½ inch from the side of your mouth. The microphone is not designed to touch your face or lips. When repositioning the Headset microphone or moving it away from your mouth, lift the boom up and toward your head. Do NOT bend it out of position or remove the entire head set. The microphone will lift up like a gate to the top of the headset / headband mechanism. You don't have to take it off.

TALK SHOW style microphone: wireless hand-held traditional microphone. Hold the microphone approximately two inches from the front of your mouth. If you are going to raise your voice, remember to move the microphone further away from your mouth about half to one inch. If you receive buzzing or loop interference the microphone is too close. If your audience cannot hear you then the microphone is not close enough or in front of your mouth.

SWING SPEAKER style microphone: corded hand-held microphone so that the speaker can dance, skip over the chord, and move around. Move with caution so that you don't trip or fall.

PODIUM HUGGER style microphone: microphone is secured to the podium. Speak directly into the microphone about three to four inches from your mouth. Position it in front of your mouth as discreetly as possible without making too much noise during the adjustment. Act as naturally as possible as you adjust the microphone. Do not block the microphone with papers, books, or folders you are reading your speech from. When possible have a sound check prior to using the microphone for your vocal performance.

ROCK STAR KISSER style microphone: microphone (corded or wireless) with pole stand. This mic and stand combination is usually for people who will speak, sing, or perform but not move around a lot. Picture your favorite Rock Star and guitar solo here. Their mic is on a stand, sometimes even secured with tape! Many are colorful and express certain artistic flair. These mics will be wireless most of the time, but once in awhile you might see a corded mic and pole. Check out some local bands and see their set-up for live performances.

© Can Stock Photo Inc. / mflippo

BOOM BOOM style microphone: microphone is an over-head mic anchored on an arm, like in a recording studio, stadium, conference room, Cathedral, university classrooms, or arena. They provide sound to a very large area of space. Boom mics are super sensitive and used to amplify a large area of both opened and closed spaces.

Have you ever noticed the mics that look like big feather dusters on the sideline of a Sunday football game on TV? Sometimes you can hear the kicker kick the pigskin from the sideline. Or the sleek plastic hooded mics, or even a long black sponge-tipped mic mounted on a mechanical arm? Boom mics will vary with location and the sound quality needed for an event.

11.3 Your Mic Type

Write about it: What style of microphones have you used in the past? What styles would you like to try out?

No matter what type of microphone you must work with, act as naturally as possible while getting situated. Try not to draw attention to the sound or height of the mic: just work through little adjustments in a graceful way when possible.

Ancient, Authentic Advice
Jesus shouted to the crowds,
"If you trust me, you are trusting not only me,
but also God who sent me."

Phase 12.0 – Performance Panache
Polishing Your Personal Speaking Style

As a speaker, you have access to a variety of performance or delivery styles, but you need to match the style with the right type of microphone. Here are four different ways to bring variety to your vocal performance.

Speaker Performance Style One: Back of Room Speaker

Begin your talk from the back of the room and work your way toward the stage, with the goal of creating an atmosphere where the audience engages from a different and unexpected point of view. This helps ease a speaker from the audience and up on to the stage.

Pros: You divert the audience's "expected" attention and can roam the audience as you gain your confidence in speaking to them. Can be very effective in small, medium and semi-large audiences and allows you to become *one* with the audience.

Cons: If you are speaking in an arena or huge audience over 250, it may not be an effective way to present your material and sometimes the sound engineers will not cooperate with this approach in a huge venue. If you are being filmed, it can be difficult for the videographer to follow you in this format. Be cautious of moving too much or too quickly, and maneuver with ease and elegance.

Preferred microphone: Lapel, lavaliere, diva, boom or cordless microphones.

Speaker Performance Style Two: Stage Roaming Speaker

This type of speaking performance is for people who want to move away from the lectern or podium. The story-telling style of speaking can be dramatized by walking while you talk. This relaxes some speakers. I encourage movement so your audience moves their eyes and you can deliver an effective talk.

Pros: Audiences stay awake longer with a moving speaker, they engage more deeply, and you create visual as well as verbal stimulation. Roaming is a very effective pattern for speaking and especially recommended for keynote speeches and comedy.

Cons: Move with purpose and caution. Quick or sudden reactions can be distracting. Sound wise, you will have to make sure that the sound engineer is aware you will be moving around. Sound check beforehand and walk the stage to make sure your volume is consistent.

Preferred microphone: Lapel, lavaliere, diva, cordless and extra LONG corded microphones.

Speaker Performance Style Three: Swing Speaker

This style can look like a jump rope session sometimes, so please use caution and don't trip yourself on the cord or get tangled up in it. You can use the cord for dramatic effect in telling a story, to break up an intense moment or add humor. If used correctly, the cord can enhance your talk and performance. Just practice it before your first appearance. You may want to have a joke prepared about corded mics to deliver as you open your talk and get situated with your mic and cord.

Pros: Gives you something to do with your hands. Provides a lead-in for you to look down and walk across the stage.

Cons: It can work against your performance if you trip or are tangled up.

Preferred mic: Corded microphones, and corded mics on a stand, typically like musicians use.

Speaker Performance Style Four: Podium Hugger

Podium huggers love the comfort of a mounted microphone. Please always adjust the mic height in a quiet manner while speaking. Avoid "testing 1-2-3" and blowing or tapping a mic when beginning a talk. Open with a short joke, quick question for the audience, or funny story to get settled with the mic position and volume adjustment.

Pros: Some speakers find comfort in being stabilized with a podium and mounted microphone.

Cons: When speakers become institutionalized by the comfort and routine of a podium and mounted mic they tend to become edgy when other options are provided without this "security". In some instances, it is difficult to read your notes if the mic is mounted on top of the podium, because you may look down and see the mic in the middle of your prose.

Preferred mic: Podium and mounted, secured microphone with or without cords.

Write about it: What speaker performance styles have you employed in the past? What styles would you like to experiment with, and why?

12.1 Speakers Who Speak to You

Begin to observe speaking performance styles of people you "listen" to on TV, a concert, play, workshop, class, or church. Take notice and check out the mic they used. How do they carry themselves while they speak? What are they wearing that is attractive or unattractive? Are they expressive? Remember, your expression is contagious. If you smile, the audience smiles. If you laugh, they laugh too. Start studying the industry and, as you observe and absorb these specifics, note what you appreciated the most from a certain speaker. We learn from one another. It is human nature.

Ancient Authentic Advice
Don't fool yourself into thinking that you are a listener
when you are anything but,
letting the Word go in one ear and out the other.
Act on what you hear!
Those who hear and don't act are like those who glance in the mirror,
walk away, and two minutes later have no idea who they are,
what they look like.

Phase 13.0 – Public Persona
Actions & Appearance Speak Louder Than Words

Our appearance shouts out to the audience many times louder than our words will. As a speaker, it is vital to inspect yourself from head to toe after obtaining your voice for your presentation. Our voice is as defining as our physical appearance or our fingerprints — no two are identical. Along with the muscles of our face and lips, we use about 14 muscles to smile and double that to frown. So remember to smile. Be sure to use your lips as you articulate. Watch yourself in the mirror. Video yourself speaking. Make these preparations part of your habits as you prepare your presentation. We will never be perfect; however, these routines do benefit our vocal performance.

Take a moment and try this:

- SMILE into a mirror.
- ARTICULATE and move your lips while you speak. How does your face look?
- PRACTICE speaking aloud and watching yourself. Could someone READ your lips?

13.1 Your Style & What to Wear Where

Just like your speech, your appearance must be polished and appropriate for your audience. We are not all rock stars or *fashionistas*, but we have to appraise our physical appearance. Dress the part, know your audience, look your best.

Exercise: Call a friend using video SKYPE and try it for thirty minutes instead of a phone call. Ask them how you look and sound.

Write about it: What feedback did they give you?

This is the time to determine what you will wear for your next speaking engagement. I suggest having at least one professional speaking outfit separate from your regular wardrobe. Ask your kids, spouse, friend, sister, and neighbor for their advice on what looks like YOU and what looks best on YOU. Invest in an image consultant to help you pick out something that flatters your shape, size, personality, and taste. Make sure you have nice shoes that are in good shape too.

Recommendations for women and men:

- **Dress the Part:** You are presenting something you are proud of and worked hard on. Dress with pride in yourself and your topic.
- **Know your audience:** Dress as professionally as you can for your audience — you want to connect with your audience. If it's a Youth Retreat wear something funky that youth might relate too. If you look like their school principal, you might lose your audience before you open your mouth. Guys and Girls can

both pull off this look: wear a nice T-shirt, casual jacket, jeans, and sneakers. If your audience is the local Professional Business People Association get out your black suit, white shirt, and red tie. Ladies should wear a navy or dark suit with closed-toe shoes.

- **Look your BEST:** When you speak, you are considered a public figure. Even if everyone is in casual dress, you should dress in a professionally casual way. Iron your outfit, wear what fits. Be comfortable with what you are wearing. Don't wear itchy wools or clingy knits.

- **Do Your Body Good:** Dye the roots of your hair if that needs fixing. Shower, buff your nails, brush and floss your teeth, use cologne, and extra deodorant. If you need to get your hair cut, make the appointment several weeks before your next gig, just in case it doesn't turn out as you planned so that you will have some time to have it redone.

- **If your image is eclectic** and you have a specific "look", that is fine — just ask others how you look before you show up on stage. Don't over-brand yourself with particular colors — it may not be something a general audience will connect with. Check out the latest trends and develop your look from that. If Goth or the 50's is your look, carry it off and just do it as well as you can. Your clothing shouts louder than you will.

Exercise: Use your laptop or video camera to video record yourself wearing your selected outfit, speaking a three-minute talk (maybe the devotional included above!). Review it. After you have settled on a video you are happy with, increase the taping time until you have a twenty-minute video that you can review and evaluate for how you look, sound, and move.

13.2 Wardrobe Watch

Write about it: What is your vision of you? Describe how you will look and sound for your next speaking opportunity.

Write about it: Given your current wardrobe, what would you wear to speak at:

- A professional or work-related conference?

- An outdoor rally?

- Your church's main worship service?

- A high school youth group retreat?

Ancient, Authentic Advice
You're beautiful from head to toe, my dear love,
beautiful beyond compare, absolutely flawless.

Phase 14.0 – Fanfare

Plans, Promo & Packaging

Well if it hasn't sunk in yet, YOU HAVE SOMETHING TO TELL and now is the time to tell it. How will you communicate your ideas, toast, manuscript, play, report, prayer, speech, story, drama, marketing plan, schedule, new job description, etc? You will need a few tools to help you reach a wide audience. The tools you need are:

1. A good introduction (face-to-face and also on your media / marketing pieces).
2. Networking connection with the world at large via social media, radio, TV, etc.
3. A marketing package that includes a website, and bio sheet / "About You" flier.

14.1 Planning Your Introduction

Let's talk about your introduction first. Your introduction should include your name, what you speak about, and an interesting fact about yourself. For example: "My name is Lisa Heidrich. My passion is to work with others in identifying their gifts while edifying and rehabilitating them as speakers. My two favorite hobbies are shopping and hanging out at the beach. I love the color purple and my fur baby is a Great Dane named Mercy."

You know the famous question, "So, tell me about yourself?" In thirty seconds or less, what would you divulge? WHO are you? What are two words that describe WHO you are? What are you passionate about? I'd like to suggest an easy way to develop what you will answer and how you will articulate it in those short conversations.

Exercise: Take a piece of paper and fold it into four sections. Now open the paper and on one side (in each square) list one word or picture that describes you, the way you see yourself. For example, why you do what you do, your education, your accolades, and what you see in your future. Now turn the paper over, and in those four boxes write down one different word or picture of how other people would describe you. You now have eight descriptive words and/or pictures. Take your eight words and sift them down to the top four. Can you make two sentences of the words you've compiled? Those two sentences are your thirty-second intro!

Allow me to feature my publisher as an example for this exercise. Front side of paper: PhD Computer Science, Publisher, Techie, Dream Finder. Back side of paper: Editor, Organizer, Encourager, Compassionate.

Therefore, when asking her, "So... tell me about you," her response could be "Hello, I am Lynellen; I have a PhD in computer Science. I am a book publisher. I have a passion for helping others complete their thoughts into concise format and assisting them in birthing their dream of a published book." I bet you can't wait to meet her, right?

Write about it: Do the exercise and write here two or three sentences using the words you compile.

_____

_____

_____

_____

_____

_____

_____

Write about it: Write out a thirty-second introduction that includes a few key points you want your fans to know about you. Now call your editor, son, daughter, spouse, friend, neighbor, or pastor and read it to them over the phone. Later read it aloud to someone in person. You got this!

Exercise: If you don't own a voice recorder of some kind, invest in one. You can also use your laptop, tablet, or smartphone. Using the device of your choice, record yourself speaking your introduction and do three "takes." Choose the best one and share it with someone for feedback.

Write about it: What feedback did you receive?

_____

_____

_____

_____

_____

_____

_____

14.2 Networking Connections

Networking in today's world requires you to connect into social media in some way. Whether you use radio, TV, Facebook, LinkedIn, Twitter, YELP, Pinterest, or something else, find one that works for you. For me, it's Twitter (follow me @LisaCHeidrich if you like), but find a way to connect beyond your local neighborhood. Facebook and Twitter are a good way to meet people with your shared interests. Start to build your following so when you are doing something new (i.e., publishing a book, magazine article, new blog, or website) you have a list of people to engage into what you are doing.

Check with your hometown newspaper, TV, and radio stations and see who interviews new authors and speakers. Use free advertising in local papers, on radio and T.V. to advertise and promote yourself as a speaker, author, workshop leader, storyteller, announcer or encourager, everyone needs one of those!

If your budget allows, invest in a Public Relations or Marketing expert to help promote you as a speaker.

NETWORK, network, network...Always ask for a referral. When you speak somewhere or simply speak with someone, always ask him or her for a referral to someone else they know who might benefit from your talk. Ask for a letter of recommendation or endorsement from three people who know you, have worked with you and are "experts" in the field or have a following that is relevant to your speaking topic.

Invest in business cards with your contact information and your photo. People are generally relational and appreciate a picture—and it is a good way to keep your face in front of someone. Always have your business cards with you and always ask people for an opportunity to speak when you meet new acquaintances. Say, "I am a speaker, I talk about such & such and would love to speak for your group, organization, business, charity, retreat, convention."

It is also important to decide that when you meet people and talk with anyone who plans events that you will inform them that you speak at conferences, retreats, rallies, banquets, etc. ASK for the business. Networking is key to obtaining venues to share your work. Informing others that you speak is step one to getting your name out there. Step two is to ask for the work. Plant the seed in people's heads that meet you as you hand them your business card. Look them in the eye and smile and say: "Here is my business card. I speak for workshops, conferences and retreats. I'd love to follow up with you and see how I can help you with your next event. Do you have a business card?" If they say no, don't freak and don't give up, just say, "Thank you for your time, it was so great to meet you (BIG

SUPER SMILE) and Oh, by the way … would you know someone else who hires speakers I could follow up with?" This is not pushy, it is just a conversation and networking with others is critical to your bookings. Don't be shy to follow your instincts. You can always pay a talent agent or event planner, but even with the pros helping you, you must still learn to open your mouth too.

Networking opportunities involve Who, What, Where, and When. Let's start with "Who."

Write about it: Begin jotting down names of people to network with for potential speaking engagements.

_____

_____

_____

_____

_____

_____

_____

_____

Who do you know that might be a good connector for you? This is someone who facilitates an introduction to people in their circle that are outside of your own social circle.

_____

_____

_____

_____

Do you know any event planners? OR anyone else who might know one? Use the web and search around.

Here are examples of the "What." Your speaking should connect with like-minded events such as Farmer's Market, Book Clubs, Nurses Day Event, Women's Retreat, Men's Conference, Rally for Youth, Cancer Survivors, Artists, Writers Guild, and Civic events.

Write about it: Write down some events that share a topic or connection with your speaking subject:

Here are examples of the "Where." Call schools, churches, country clubs, community centers ask if they are looking for workshop or retreat leaders. Start somewhere and keep a list of who you call and what you sent to each new contact. I suggest your information packet contain a letter of introduction, your "About You" info sheet, endorsements, and business card.

Write about it: Write down some places you will call this week.

Here are examples of the "When." Have a passion for kid's safety on Halloween? Remember to contact Moms groups and schools prior to October 31 to schedule your info session. Early May events include: Mother's Day, Nurses day, and the National Day of Prayer. Get on the internet and search for celebration days. You'll be surprise to find out how many different kinds of "National Day of _____" there are! Call where these events are located: Churches, Hospitals, Library, Restaurants and Community rooms, and ask if they need a speaker. Call the local Rodeo, Auctions, Sports arenas, and High Schools, and ask if they need announcers for sporting events. Volunteer to read aloud at a bookstore, Children's Hospital, or Nursing Home. This is a great way to practice speaking and network beyond your daily routine.

Many event organizers book a year or more in advance but there are some who have last minute openings and might even create an opportunity for you if your timing is right and your pitch is effective. Ask for the business and tell everyone you meet: "I speak at...... (fill in the blank)." You are responsible to get your information out there and SHOUT!

GIVE a little. It is totally legal to give a little for FREE. Starting out, you might speak for certain events and opportunities just for practice and exposure. All those freebies turn into potential paying work down the road.

Write about it: What days or times of the year are relevant to your speaking topic?

_____

_____

_____

_____

_____

_____

Exercise: Volunteer to do an announcement for an event or concert in your community. If you are near a local radio station, ask if you can practice doing a "30 second spot." Then ask if they will send you a copy via electronic file (wav file, mp3 file, etc.).

14.3 Marketing One-Liners

Networking is just one aspect of promoting yourself as a speaker. You'll also need some marketing items. You'll need to write up, offline, a simple marketing plan to get your face and your message OUT THERE. Let's talk about some elements of that marketing package.

Your first marketing task is to create a mission statement. Think about marketing phrases from successful businesses:

Nike: "Just DO It"

Delta: "We Earn Our Wings Every Day"

Coke: "Open Happiness"

Lisa Heidrich: "I edify people and rehabilitate speakers"

Write about it: Write out your mission statement here. Share it with a few people for feedback. Then memorize the final version.

If you have been completing the exercises in the previous chapters, you have recorded yourself speaking several different times. Now you need to create a recording that will be your audio demonstration for your marketing kit. Record a testimony or longer presentation and have it available as an electronic copy, CD, or tape. Sometimes certain types of venues (retreats, conferences, and workshops) have committees that review a speaker prior to hire and want a full performance of your work.

Your next marketing item to create is a demonstration video. Compile a 3-4 minute video of yourself to send out to potential places to speak. What should you talk about in the video? Speak on a subject of interest, provide a devotional, or give statistics about what you are passionate about. Let this be an introduction, a cameo performance, a teaser, a trailer, and an appetizer of you as a speaker.

You'll also need a Letter of Introduction that explains who you are and why you are sending your demo CD to the recipient. Here is an example Letter of Introduction. Use this as a model to write your own.

Introducing Lisa Heidrich, Speaker, Author & Teacher
for your next conference, retreat or seminar!

Thank you for allowing me to share this presentation portfolio with you. Enclosed please find:
• Personal Information Sheet
• Program Topics
• Endorsements
• Contact Information
I warmly welcome your feedback and hope these info sheets are useful in selecting me as a speaker for your next event. As a Christ Follower, my heart's desire and spiritual gifts drive me to share the Gospel and God's Promises. As a Registered Nurse, I have a passion for helping women understand health issues in a sensible and endearing manner. Combined together, I want to be part of changing this world for Jesus and touching women's lives.
Choosing a speaker certainly takes time and consideration. It would be an honor to minister to your group. The goal the Lord has placed on my heart is to make each event encouraging, practical, inspirational, and fun as well as to introduce new audiences to what God has called me to do. I appreciate your reviewing my enclosed information and look forward to hearing from you soon. I pray you will consider me for your next event and look forward to meeting your group.

Until then,
May the Son shine in your eyes and the joy of our Lord in your heart.

Lisa Heidrich, RN, CCM, CHP
Phone #
www.LisaHeidrich.com
"We thank you Lord, we thank you! Your Name is our favorite Word"! ~ Psalm 75:1

Next, you need a website that focuses on your speaking career. If you don't have the skills, hire someone. My website is http://www.LisaHeidrich.com and was developed by graphic artist Pam Cherry (pjcherry_1@yahoo.com) and also eKnowSys, Inc. (http://www.eknowsys.com), so if you like how mine looks, contact them. On your website, begin a blog or start a Vlog (video blog). Put together a webpage with your picture, the introduction you created in the exercise above, and details on how others might connect with you. Add a vocal recording to your web page.

Develop an "About You" flier, which includes the following elements:

- Your name — either your real name or your alias / stage name. Whichever you will use as your public persona. Your name is your number one marketing tool and you want people to remember you.
- A recent head-and-shoulders photo of you, taken by a professional.
- Your PASSION statement (2-3 sentences identifying what you are passionate about).
- Your MISSION statement (1-2 sentences identifying what you are excited about and defines your goal).
- Your contact information (including cell phone, website address, and social media details for Facebook, Twitter, etc.).
- Your relevant education and/or experience.
- Five-Six KEY topics you speak about, or how you are defined as a person.
- One or more short endorsements from someone noteworthy and who supports what you are doing.

How should you lay out these elements on the page? Be creative! Will you format your flier as folded brochure, a one-page info sheet, a half page marketing postcard, or poster sized? Color or black and white? Your "About You" flier should reflect who you are as a speaker. Dare to be different and unique!

Place your photo anywhere on the flier ... top, middle, bottom, a corner ... wherever you like it best. Make sure your contact information is either at the top or across the bottom. Your name should be mentioned FIRST & LAST. At least twice on your flier.

Here are two examples of the "About You" fliers that I use. They are in full color in my marketing kit, using my favorite purple as a theme color. For this book, they are black and white. What do you like about them? Make notes to include those elements in your own piece. What do you not like about them, and how would you make changes to make the flier more "you"?

As you begin working on your marketing package "to-do" list, check off each item you produce:

_____ Obtain a photo / headshot of you.

_____ Set up a website.

_____ Print business cards (with your picture on them).

_____ Create an "About You" info sheet.

_____ Write your Letter of Introduction.

_____ Record your demo CD.

_____ Record your demo video.

_____ Brainstorm networking opportunities (WHO, WHAT, WHERE, WHEN).

_____ ASK for the business.

Lisa Heidrich, RN, CCM, CHP

Speaker, Author, Voice-Over Artist

Lisa's passion is to share the **HOPE** of Jesus with every generation, pray profusely with no boundaries, be an Activist for the Body of Christ, help others discover unique gifts and talents, develop your voice for Him and watch you explode into who God created "YOU to **BE**."

- International Speaker and Prayer Leader
- Body of Christ Activist
- Author
- Global Conversationalist
- Freelance Writer
- Voice-Over Artist

She will energize your passion for truth, real truth, God's truth!

In Lisa's calling:

As an **Evangelist**, Lisa shares her testimony **Finding Hope In a Hope-Less World**, and teaches others how to share their journey of success, sanctification & sanity.

As a **Prayer Intercessor and Prayer Leader**, she leads prayer retreats, devotions, one-on-one prayer coaching, and workshops.

As a **Teacher**, she shares REAL TRUTH from God's Word and will assist you in discovering how you are wired with unique gifts and talents.

As a **Speaking Coach**, she will help you find your voice, get over barriers and share your story with confidence.

As a **Champion**, she delights in seeing others explode into WHO God created them to be.

"When you invite Lisa to speak you are getting a power-packed, power-filled woman of God! She brings knowledge, grace and above all, laughter that is much needed in today's culture. Each woman will leave having encountered the living God!" ~Shari Brandel, Proverbs 31 Speaker

Lisa is a graduate of.....P31 Ministries "She Speaks"

Lisa is available for
seminars, conferences, retreats and banquets.
She would love to assist you with your next event.

Contact Information

www.lisaheidrich.com

(704) 953-6993

t:@LisaCHeidrich

e:lisalisa114@gmail.com

Author of Speaking Confidence
published by Chalfont Press, Inc (debut Fall 2012)

Speaker, Author, Voice-Over Artist

LISA HEIDRICH

Lisa's passion is to share the **HOPE** of Jesus with every generation, pray profusely with no boundaries, be an Activist for the Body of Christ, help others discover unique gifts and talents, find a nd develop your voice for Him and watch you explode into who God created YOU to **BE**

- International Speaker and Prayer Leader
- Body of Life Activist
- Author

- Global Conversationalist
- Freelance Writer
- Voice - Over Artist

She will energize your passion for truth, real truth, God's truth!

In Lisa's calling:

As and **Evangelist**, Lisa shares her testimony **Finding Hope In a Hope-Less World**, and teaching others how to share their journey of success, sanctification & sanity.

As a **Prayer Intercessor and Prayer Leader**, she leads prayer retreats, devotions, one -on-one prayer coaching, and workshops.

As a **Teacher**, she shares REAL TRUTH from God's Word and will assist you in discovering how you are wired with unique gifts and talents.

As a **Speaking Coach**, she will help you find your voice, get over barriers and share your story with confidence.

As a **Champion**, she delights in seeing others explode in WHO God created them to be.

"When you invite Lisa to speak you are getting a power-packed, power-filled woman of God! She brings knowledge, grace and above all, laughter that is much needed in today's culture. Each woman will leave having encountered the living God!" ~Shari Brandel, Proverbs 31 Speaker

Contact Information : Lisa Heidrich

Lisa is available for seminars, conferences, retreats and banquets. She would love to assit you with your next event.

www.lisaheidrich.com   (704) 953-6993   t:@LisaCHeidrich   e:lisalisa114@gmail.com

Gather together your speaker package. Include your letter of introduction, demo audio CD, demo video DVD, recommendation letters, and business cards, topics you speak on, published works, website address, phone number, "About You" flier with picture, and a list of other places you have spoken.

Your efforts at self-promotion, networking, and marketing should lead to speaking opportunities. You might start doing pro bono work, but most likely your goal is to derive some income from your speaking. Here are my tips on being paid to speak.

1. **Speaking fees should be negotiated in advance.** I recommend that you check out other speakers in your region who speak on the same topic as you for a guideline. If you must travel to the venue, consider those expenses and arrange for them beforehand. Speakers receive all kinds of honorarium from gifts to thousands of dollars. Google "public speaker pay rates" and discover a whole wide world of ranges.

2. **As a beginning speaker** with a thirty minute presentation for a local venue, don't be afraid to ask for anywhere between $75.00-$100.00.

3. **Retreat speakers that are just starting out** and speaking for two days can range from $400 to $600.00 to present two to three times.

4. **Experienced Keynote speakers** with a thirty to ninety minute presentation can receive from $500 to $2500.00, depending on the event.

5. **Full time, professional speakers, and celebrities** can ask for rates anywhere from $5000.00 to $150,000.00 and up for their venues.

6. **You can always simply ask them to pay their "usual and customary honorarium"** or even ask what their budget allows for the event. Or you can say, "I will let God tell YOU how you will bless me." Or ask if they will take up a "love offering."

7. **If you are promoting your book,** always ask for a table at the back of the room where you can sell merchandise. Sometimes you will receive more revenue from table sales than the actual honorarium.

Ancient Authentic Advice
Was I fickle when I intended to do this?
Or do I make my plans in a worldly manner
so that in the same breath I say both
"Yes, yes" and "No, no"?

Phase 15.0 – Applause
Expectations, Experiences & Ending Thoughts

Even if your expectation is not to go out and change the world, I can't wait to hear how this journey with me has touched your life and I invite you to keep in touch. I'd love to hear from you. Your words matter to me, so know that in advance. I am impressed that you now have the beginning tools to share your dream verbally with others. That's an accomplishment!

May the journals in these pages remind you of your beginning experiences and demonstrate your growth as you move forward. You made it. I pray it has helped you in your search for your speaking confidence. How have you grown? Have you taken a step forward, even if just a tiny step forward? Just as a momma bird teaches her birdies to fly, now is the time to jump out and experience what you have been speculating about, obsessing over and preparing for. May your glide out of the nest be one you never regret or forget. You are ready. Your audience is waiting. You have the tools. Now is the time. GO speak, confidently.

As you speak confidence into others, it builds you up as a person. It is totally free and all it takes is a moment and a breath to share and breathe life into another person. You are brilliant. May all the words you speak inspire and encourage others. This is a conscious choice that yields return one hundred fold. It is the best boomerang life can offer us. Godspeed to you.

As we reach the end of this book, allow me to summarize my best list of speaking tips:

- Always be ready and standing when you are being introduced to speak. Getting up from a table or seated position is awkward. Be up and ready to walk up front.
- Always use a microphone when possible. Most professional

speakers use a microphone. Do not try to shout or yell your speech.

- Bring more than one copy of your talk. I suggest you also send your speech to someone else attending the event in case you lose your copies or misplace them.

- Do not try new colognes, shaving creams, face creams, makeup, vitamins, medications, laundry detergent, new dry cleaners, anything internal or external (including foods, spices, drinks) before a presentation — if you have a rash or an allergic reaction it might make for a tough day as a speaker.

- Get a good night's rest as far in advance as you can, especially the night before a talk. If you need help falling asleep, try prayer, meditation, or medication from your doctor — but try the meds before you talk — make sure you know how you react to them and how you feel the next day. You don't want to be foggy or feeling hung-over before a talk.

- Arrive early and get a sense of the room layout. Walk around, say hello to people, and chitchat to break the ice and warm up your voice. Chew a piece of gum or breath mint prior to talking with people and have a glass or bottle of water handy — get your vocal chords nice and wet before speaking.

- Keep a checklist of everything you need, especially if traveling for a talk. Have your outfit ready and bring two pairs of shoes. Remember most speakers STAND, and depending on the length of your presentation, you may want to invest in some comfortable shoes.

- Dress the part. Look professional for your talk, your style and your audience. Wear what looks great on you and you feel comfortable wearing. YES, everyone will be looking at you and you look dynamite!

- When possible arrive early enough for a "sound check" just so you know what type of microphone is available and you can get a chance to hear how you sound, feel familiar with the placement of the mike, and where you might place your notes, iPad, tablet, notebook, etc.

- Bring a watch or set your phone timer, and be cognizant of the time. You want to stay on time, honor your audience's time and also do what you were invited to do. If you were hired to talk 15 minutes, don't talk 16. Stay on time for what you were asked to do. You are not responsible for the people before you or after you. If the schedule is running late, that is up to the Emcee or producer of the event to apologize and gain back lost time. You were invited to speak for a certain time and that is what is expected.

- Have a hanky or tissue handy. If you break into a sweat, tears, or have a hot flash it is totally acceptable to wipe your eyes, nose, face, or mouth (when needed) as you speak. Be as diplomatic as possible, but don't let anything drip down your face or forehead.

- Remember to look at your audience and everyone in the audience—if that is freaky then focus on something beyond your audience but looks like you are looking at them. LOOK UP and out to your audience, don't look down on them. Keep your eyes upward and outward whatever you decide to look at. Do notice your audience and remember no one gives classes on audiences — they don't realize that they have to smile, nod, or acknowledge what you are saying. If you smile at them, they might actually smile back. You keep a pleasant look as much as you can.

- Give your audience time to respond to what you say or ask them. This is important for humor. When you say something funny, give them 7 seconds to GET IT — count to yourself as you laugh and look around the room. It cues your audience that it was OK to laugh at what you said. YOU are in charge.

- Always thank your audience, anyone who invited you or promoted you at the end of your talk. Everyone appreciates a grateful speaker.
- Ask for evaluations whenever possible so that you can use that feedback to improve your future speeches. Offer your own evaluation form so that you get responses on specific areas.

15.1 Tracking Your Next Six Speaking Engagements

I am including extra pages here for you to record your next six speaking engagements. May these journals serve you well in recording your vocal performances and develop into a habit you will keep throughout your career as a magnificent public speaker. It works to have your thoughts and feedback recorded so you can stay in a continuum of development in your speaking. Keep a record, look back, learn what worked and what you want to tweak. It is truly an ongoing process that will return to you multiplied what you put into it.

Watch, your audience and fans are expecting you.

I applaud you now, for Speaking Confidence.

15.2 Gig Journal

Copies may be used only by written permission from the publisher.

Speaking Engagement #1

PLACE:

TOPIC:

WHAT I remember:

WHAT I forgot:

The Audience's response:

How did your audience LOOK?

My phobia level now:
(Rate it 1-10; one being low fear, ten being high fear.)

Speaking Engagement #2

PLACE:

TOPIC:

WHAT I remember:

WHAT I forgot:

The Audience's response:

How did your audience LOOK?

My phobia level now:
(Rate it 1-10; one being low fear, ten being high fear.)

Speaking Engagement #3

PLACE:

TOPIC:

WHAT I remember:

WHAT I forgot:

The Audience's response:

How did your audience LOOK?

My phobia level now:
(Rate it 1-10; one being low fear, ten being high fear.)

Speaking Engagement #4

PLACE:

TOPIC:

WHAT I remember:

WHAT I forgot:

The Audience's response:

How did your audience LOOK?

My phobia level now:
(Rate it 1-10; one being low fear, ten being high fear.)

Speaking Engagement #5

PLACE:

TOPIC:

WHAT I remember:

WHAT I forgot:

The Audience's response:

How did your audience LOOK?

My phobia level now:
(Rate it 1-10; one being low fear, ten being high fear.)

Speaking Engagement #6

PLACE:

TOPIC:

WHAT I remember:

WHAT I forgot:

The Audience's response:

How did your audience LOOK?

My phobia level now:
(Rate it 1-10; one being low fear, ten being high fear.)

Ancient, Authentic Advice
I am glad I can have complete confidence in you.

Phase 16.0 – Rhetoric Resources
Speaker Tools

16.1 Speaker Websites to Visit

One site I like to recommend is Toastmasters International. You can check out their website at: www.toastmasters.org

You might also want to look into the National Speakers Association at : www.nsa.org

For information about microphone setup, visit http://www.nuance.com/naturallyspeaking/customer-portal/documentation/userguide/chapter2/ug_chapter2_microphone_setup.pdf

For speaking training and speaking coaching, visit www.LisaHeidrich.com

16.2 Speaker Evaluation Tool

Copies may be used only by written permission from the publisher.

Talk Title: _____

Speaker Name: _____

Was this your first time hearing this speaker? Yes / No

How will you use the key points from today's conference?

What did you enjoy best? (use back for additional comments and feedback)

What could have been done better?

In what areas would you like additional teaching? (Circle ALL that apply)

   Evangelism Leadership   Prayer Leadership

   Community Leadership   Other:

Rate the program in the following areas (with 5 being BEST and 1 being the WORST)

REGISTRATION: 1 2 3 4 5

TOPICS: 1 2 3 4 5

SESSION LENGTH: 1 2 3 4 5

FOOD: 1 2 3 4 5

LOCATION: 1 2 3 4 5

SPEAKER: 1 2 3 4 5

Please provide your name and email below to receive info about upcoming events (PLEASE PRINT CLEARLY)

Name:

Phone: EMAIL:

~Thank you for joining us for this event!~

16.3 Speaker Evaluation Form

Copies may be used only by written permission from the publisher.

Speaker Name: _____

Was this your first time hearing this speaker? Yes / No

Were your expectations met? Yes / No

Would you listen to this speaker again? Yes / No

Would you invite a friend next time? Yes / No

How did you hear about this conference?

Please evaluate the speaker in the following categories, with 5 being BEST and 1 being the WORST.

EYE CONTACT: 1 2 3 4 5   TOPIC: 1 2 3 4 5

SESSION LENGTH: 1 2 3 4 5   SOUND: 1 2 3 4 5

APPEARANCE: 1 2 3 4 5   TIMING: 1 2 3 4 5

HUMOR: 1 2 3 4 5   CONFIDENCE: 1 2 3 4 5

ENTHUSIASM: 1 2 3 4 5   CLARITY: 1 2 3 4 5

PERFORMANCE: 1 2 3 4 5

What did you enjoy best from this Speaker? (use back for additional comments and feedback)

What could this Speaker do next time to improve their presentation?

Please provide your name and email below to receive info about up-coming events (PLEASE PRINT CLEARLY)

Name:

Phone: EMAIL:

~Thank you for joining us for this event!~

16.4 Speaker Checklist

Copies may be used only by written permission from the publisher.

1. Address, map, and clear directions of where your venue is located.
2. Phone number of contact person.
3. Date and time of the presentation.
4. Type of audience / theme / dress / attire.
5. Know how long you will need to travel to get there (accounting for traffic / road construction / time of day).
6. Fill up with a *full* tank of gas, if driving.
7. Ask where you should park upon arrival and ask whether you need a pass or special parking instructions.
8. If taking public transportation, have a current schedule, transfer, pass and ID ready in advance.
9. Clean and Ready Outfit.
10. Comfortable shoes (bring an extra pair).
11. Local currency, if in a foreign country.
12. Passport, if in a foreign country.
13. Ladies: makeup and female stuff..just in case.
14. Breath mints, gum, hard candy.
15. WATER. Have some ready and available.
16. Cell phone and charger.
17. Watch or other timing device.
18. Eyeglasses, especially as a back-up if you wear contact lenses.
19. Eyeglass cleaner & wiping cloth.
20. Eye drops.
21. Laptop/tablet computer.
22. Laptop/tablet power cable.
23. Sound check of microphone and sound system at the venue.
24. If bringing your own microphone, don't forget it!

25. Extra batteries.
26. Small speakers as back-up if your presentation has sound.
27. Multi-socket electric power strip and/or extension cord.
28. Converter plugs for electrical equipment if speaking in a foreign country.
29. For Mac users, an adapter to enable you to connect your computer to a beamer. The standard one is the VGA adapter but there are others, so be sure that you have the right one.
30. USB back-up copy of presentation. (For Mac users, if your presentation is on Keynote and your computer freezes, Keynote will not work on a PC. Consider having a Power Point version as well, if practicable.)
31. Remote control for your slide presentation.
32. Speaking notes, if needed.
33. JUMP Drive.
34. Hard copy of presentation slides (or key ones) in case equipment fails.
35. Hard copy of thumb nails of slides for quick reference.
36. Your written introduction for the person introducing you to the audience.
37. Props.
38. Tissues or hanky.
39. Colored markers for a flip chart.
40. Colored markers for a white board.
41. Notepad.
42. Pens / Pencils / Highlighters.
43. Books to sell in the back of the room. Be sure to order in advance from Publisher and see if they can be shipped directly to your venue contact.
44. Any back table items you will sell or need shipped in advance.
45. Reference material. If you get a question at the end of the presen-

tation and do not know the answer, you might be able to find it after the session and speak to the person who asked the question.

46. Background material from your host (programme, list of participants, etc.).

47. Handouts related to the presentation.

48. Promotional material for yourself or your company / organization.

49. Samples.

50. Business cards.

51. Evaluations if you wish to get feedback or venue requires that.

52. Preferred energy food or snack.

53. Medication if needed. Keep aspirin, ibuprofen or acetaminophen handy for last minute headaches.

54. Spare shirt and tie or blouse if giving a speech after a meal. (You never know when you are going to spill something.)

55. Stain remover pen for any small food spills.

56. Umbrella.

57. Video camera and stand if filming yourself.

58. A positive frame of mind! Even though you have lots to remember, don't let it detract from your commitment to be fully engaged with your audience.

59. Words of confidence to remind yourself: YOU CAN DO THIS.

60. Phone number for your emergency contact.

61. Flight information, ticket, boarding pass, itinerary

62. Coat or jacket for bad weather.

63. Cardigan sweater for chilly rooms.

64. Recording device if recording your talk.

65. Hand lotion.

66. Breath spray, mouth wash.

67. Hair spray.

68. Tooth brush and tooth paste.

69. Tooth floss, tooth pick.

70. Your "About You" flyer / one-sheet / bio sheet.

71. Website information.

72. Twitter, Facebook, Pinterest info.

73. Extra hose / tights.

74. Sign Up sheet to add names and emails to your list of contacts for future book sales, blogs, emails, newsletters. Use this as appropriate for your audience.

75. Clip board for sing up sheet.

76. Several pens just for the sign up sheet.

77. Bring your confidence.

Ancient Authentic Advice
"I'm speaking to you as dear friends.
Don't be bluffed into silence or insincerity
by the threats of religious bullies.
True, they can kill you, but then what can they do?
There's nothing they can do to your soul, your core being.
Save your fear for God, who holds your entire life
—body and soul — in His hands.

16.5 Ancient Authentic Advice References

Phase 1.0 Communicating: Psalm 39:1-3 (The Message)

Phase 2.0 Speaking Phobia: Hebrews 13:6 (The Message)

Phase 3.0 Audience Authenticity: Mark 1:27 (NLT)

Phase 4.0 Revision of Rejection: Romans 3:2-6 (The Message)

Phase 5.0 Self Strengths: Matthew 6:21 (NIV)

Phase 6.0 Figuratively Speaking: Galatians 6:4-5 (The Message)

Phase 7.0 Transformative Narrative: Matthew 13:34 (The Message)

Phase 8.0 Vocal Performance: Matthew 12:34 (The Message)

Phase 9.0 Respiration: Ezekiel 37:9 (NLT)

Phase 10.0 Presentation Styles: Proverbs 18:21 (AMP Bible)

Phase 11.0 Articulation Amplification: John 12:44 (NLT)

Phase 12.0 Performance Panache: James 1: 22-24 (The Message)

Phase 13.0 Public Persona: Song of Solomon 4:7 (The Message)

Phase 14.0 Fanfare: 1 Corinthians 1:17 (NIV)

Phase 15.0 Applause: 2 Corinthians 7:16 (NIV)

Phase 16.0 Rhetoric References: Luke 12:4-5 (The Message)

ABOUT THE AUTHOR

Lisa Heidrich, RN, CCM, CHP, is a registered nurse, nursing instructor, international speaker, speaking coach, ministry director, Bible study teacher, prayer intercessor, voice-over artist and freelance writer with over 20 years experience in public speaking. Lisa serves Stonecroft Ministries as a speaker and Divisional Field Director. She is a Proverbs 31 "She Speaks" and Christian Communicators Conference graduate. Her passion is to teach God's Truth, speak His words, pray and connect others to their ultimate vocal performance. She is an advocate for the Body of Christ and believes everyone has gifts and talents for utmost adoration to Jesus. The things of this world are temporary and true freedom comes only in realizing your true identity and eternity. Religion will never save us from ourselves, but relationship will.

She advises that when we speak, we must aim to instill and demonstrate Speaking Confidence not only in ourselves but also to encourage and ignite the hearts and voices of others.

Communicator, Coach, Catalyst, Connector.
Edifying people and rehabilitating speakers.

Psalm 75:1 "We thank you God, we thank you. Your NAME is our favorite word. Your mighty deeds are all we have to brag about." (The Message)

Lisa is available for your next conference or retreat. Please contact her at: www.LisaHeidrich.com
Twitter: @LisaCHeidrich
Email: LisaLisa114@gmail.com